# Parables from the Prairie

# PARABLES FROM THE PRAIRIE

*How an Admiral Was
Trained on Dry Land*

**DENNIS A. JONES**

Infusionmedia
Lincoln, Nebraska

Infusionmedia

140 North 8th Street #214

Lincoln, NE 68508-1353

infusion.media

ISBN: 978-0-9970155-0-8

LCCN: 2017938363

10 9 8 7 6 5 4 3 2 1

First Edition

# Dedication

My wife, Janet, was not around during my childhood days, of course, but she has heard my stories, many, many, many times. In fact, she deserves much credit for smiling and nodding lovingly as I and my classmates relive our childhood at every high school reunion. She only occasionally remarks that some story had a different ending than when it was told a prior time.

Janet gets all the credit for the publishing of this book because it was her idea that I should record these memories. It may have been her way of getting me out from underfoot, but I love her for prodding me. This has been great fun.

Special thanks also to a great friend and listener—my dog Tallie.

Over a three-year period, Tallie took up residence under my desk during every rainy day as I recorded this manuscript. She would raise her head and acknowledge my happiness every time I would giggle about a memory. I would explain to her what had taken place so many years ago and what I was going to say about it. She always seemed to understand and approve.

# Contents

# Preface

Psychologists and psychiatrists have always known that where you were raised, how you lived, the quality of your teachers, and what you were taught as a child is ultra-important in how you turn out as an adult. Everything from what church you attend now to what you discuss with your family at the dinner table and what foods you enjoy are a result of that time when everyone, including your parents, didn't think you were listening. Your adult lifestyle and thought processes are greatly affected by the area of the country that you were raised in, and even by the size of the community where your family lived. There is no doubt that Midwesterners think differently than those folks who were raised on the coasts of our country or in large urban areas. Coastal folks might refer to those of us that were raised in the middle of the country as "quaint," or "down home," or "nice folks." Heck, that sounds fine to me. However, what they are probably thinking is that we are a bunch of hick, Bible-thumping morons who are downright unsophisticated. My wife, who is a product of the liberal east and who is my best friend, has her own subtle way of letting me know that she and I think differently. She refers to me as a product of a "square state." She has never been able to explain if that means that I'm square in my thought process or if that means that Midwestern states have a more defined geometric shape. Perhaps it's best if I do not know.

I'm convinced that some folks are just jealous, and besides, I don't care what they think because I was just being a kid and having fun when I grew up in the greatest part of the country. Later in life, I would learn that the best sailors that I had in my crew came from the Midwest. They had a more dedicated work habit, they were more ethical, and I'm convinced that their ability to adjust and get the job done was because they had my kind of childhood.

Today that influence of family, the location of my hometown, and the memories of many years ago still invade my daily routine. The mannerisms that I display in my business dealings are those of my mom and dad. I even read roadside signs, out loud, like my mother used to do when we went on automobile trips. I can't pass a deer crossing sign without saying, "Deer zing." It drove me crazy back in my youth, and it drives my passengers crazy now. But, I still do it. The things that bothered my father politically bother me. Even though everything changes, nothing changes.

Recently, I attended a high school reunion and was surprised to find out that I had attended high school with a bunch of old people. But it was even worse than that. Throughout the reunion festivities, it was obvious that these old people were acting just like they did when they were in high school. The same cliques developed during the evening. The jokesters continued their teenage pranks; the smart folks avoided those who were considered less smart, even though some of the less smart were now very successful captains of industry. People called each other by their childhood nicknames. Old romances attempted reignition, but luckily without liftoff. And for me, I realized that even though I had been relatively successful in the intervening years, I still felt a bit inferior when around various classmates— even the less successful. This was crazy, but it was happening, and we all felt comfortable reverting to the personalities of our adolescent days. I decided then and there that I needed to record what I could remember of my early years, before I could no longer remember them. I'm sure that day will arrive! Some of the stories you will read in the following chapters are about nutty things, some about near-illegal episodes, some about crazy and stupid stunts, and others that I hope will warm your heart.

I needed to know that I had a record of the events that had caused me to be the way I am. A record that I could read in the later years, to help me remember the good-old days.

As I transcribed my youthful events, it concerned me that if my children and grandchildren read this book, it would confirm their suspicion that their dad and grandpa was a troublemaker child, and that is the reason that he is now a crazy old man. Therefore, let me state, kids, *do not try to replicate these events*. They were performed by people who, at the time, thought they were professionals.

As a disclaimer, I acknowledge that my memory is not perfect. Additionally, some parts of this treatise are out-and-out lies. The readers will need to decide for themselves what is just too hard to swallow. That being said, every event that is described is an event that actually happened, with a little bit of Tom Sawyer-like embellishment, of course.

Most of what I have recorded comes from my personal memory bank, but there were times that I clearly needed help in piecing together the whole story. It was during those times that I turned to my sisters and classmates who also lived through some of the same events. It is to them that I owe a huge debt of gratitude for their help and patience as I attempted to pull the truth, or near truth, together.

I must also admit that as I wrote, I became concerned that I may be revealing parts of other people's lives that they would prefer remain hidden. As such, in many cases I provided copies of pertinent chapters to those people who were mentioned or referred to, and then waited anxiously for their comments before proceeding. I was always pleasantly surprised by the helpful hints and warm comments of enthusiasm that I received, indicating to me that these folks were also enjoying a journey down memory lane. One answer that I received is memorable—"Well, I'm not admitting it, but that could have happened."

In the beginning, I really did not have a clear idea of what I wanted to write or how to go about recording my thoughts. I only knew that I wanted to capture some of the vignettes that stood out in my childhood memory. Early on, it became clear that I was not writing a continuous story; I was simply penning a series of short stories that did not necessarily follow a pattern—snapshots of memorable events. Much later in the writing cycle, it occurred to me that I had not even thought about a title for what I was remembering. I wanted the title to be something about "growing up" in a wonderful place or about the "differences" in how we live our lives today, but capturing that thought in a title eluded me.

It was not until I started reading and rereading each chapter that it came to me that I had not written about adventuresome memories or just plain fun events. I had recorded events that had influenced my life. As I read, I realized that every chapter had a childhood lesson to be learned, and that lesson had affected the way I had matured and operated my entire adult life.

What I have recorded, and I hope all will learn from, is a series of my own personal "parables," simple stories used to illustrate a moral or spiritual lesson learned. Enjoy.

## CHAPTER 1

## Johnny and Vera

———————

One cannot write a book about one's childhood without first talking a little about Mom and Dad. We did not have very much in the financial area while I was growing up, but on the other hand, I didn't know it. We lived in a metropolis of three thousand people, and even though I was aware that there were folks who had more money than we did, it just did not seem to matter. The entire town was basically an agrarian society. If the farmers did well, the town's population had a reasonable year. If it was a bad year for the crops, the town's survival was an issue. This was nothing more than fact for many Midwestern farm towns.

My mom was the twin daughter of Kansas farmers and a wonderful homemaker. Mom was a tiny lady but full of enormous energy. She never went anywhere unless it was at high speed. Like all mothers at that time, my mom never worked outside the household. That changed when I went away to college, but for me, Mom was always home. Mom's day started early, as she always made breakfast before Dad went to work and I went to school.

My schools were never more than a half mile away, and every day I would come home for lunch. Even during some of the nastiest Nebraska snowstorms, I would go home for some warm food. Looking back, I think one of the reasons for going home for lunch was that it was cheaper than eating at school. Dad would also be there, and we would all sit down together. There was a lot of food—that was one thing we never skimped on—but we ate quickly so we could be on our way back to school and work in a timely manner. Mom, who sprinted around the kitchen, seemed to be too busy to take part in lunchtime discussions, but Dad wanted to discuss sports. It seems to me that I was constantly trying to make a sports team that Dad considered important. The evening meal was served at five thirty sharp. At least, that is when Mom and Dad ate. If I was at a sports practice, Mom made sure that I had the same warm meal when I arrived home. In fact, I have very few memories of my mother where she wasn't in the kitchen, running around like a woman on a mission. That was just the way it was!

My dad was the son of a carpenter and was a big-city guy. At least a big-city guy in relative terms. Fairbury was the county seat of Jefferson County and, as a result, was considered big. He had been a good athlete in high school and was the starting center on the only undefeated football team in the town's history. His nickname was "Mad Dog," which brings a smile to my face because he only weighed 135 pounds when he was in high school. However, the stories I have heard led me to believe that he could be quite mean on the football field and that he deserved the moniker. I saw some of that—should we say *toughness*—while I was growing up. For me, Dad could be rough to deal with, and there were many times back then that I thought he was being unfair. Today I think differently.

Dad was drafted into the Army Air Corps during the later stages of World War II, and he was stationed in Bisbee, Arizona, for his training. Dad would have loved to be a daring pilot, but as a draftee, the closest he got to an aircraft was as an aviation mechanic.

He complained a lot about how many times he and his buddies had to fix aircraft that student pilots had damaged during hard landings. The Army was training pilots for various European countries, like Poland and Yugoslavia, at the time, and the language barrier could be challenging. Dad said that sometimes the control tower had trouble explaining to the foreign students that putting the wheels down was important to the landing sequence. Dad did a lot of work on crash landings.

Mom and I remained with her folks on the Kansas farm while Dad underwent the initial basic training period, and then we joined him in Arizona. I'm sure that I had an enjoyable trip, all the time being excited about seeing my dad again. However, today when I think about that 1,081.2-mile trip in a 1937 Plymouth, with a three-year-old, I have a different opinion. It must have been quite an adventure for a young mother who had never been very far from the farm.

I recall the tears on everyone's faces as we stood in front of the old farmhouse, trying to hug each other just one more time. The car was full to the top, and, of course, Grandma had packed us enough food for the entire trip because Mom was afraid to stop.

It had rained the night before, so the dirt roads were a quagmire as we left the farm. There was some discussion about Grandpa having to tow us with the tractor out to the main road, but that was not necessary. However, the muddy roads prevented us from traveling very fast, and that turned out to be a good thing.

After we had gone about ten miles, we could see an old Model A Ford chasing us at a speed that Fords of that day were not supposed to go. Grandpa was honking and waving out the window as he approached. It turns out that we had forgotten my most prized possession, and if I had discovered it missing sooner, there would have been a whole lot of screaming going on. My favorite stuffed animal, Lamby the sheep, was now on his way to Arizona as well.

For a kid, Arizona was a paradise because it was just rocks, dirt, cactus, and neat places to play cowboys and Indians. But my guess is that it was hot and miserable for the adults. The military base had been carved out of the wilderness and was one of those places that had been constructed at the beginning of the war. The buildings were nothing more than Quonset huts and structures with paper-thin walls. No heating was required, and air conditioning did not exist. Our house was small and was one of about twenty homes that all looked the same and were all attached in a row. It was nothing but a long Quonset-type building with a bunch of doors. Our front porch was about three feet by three feet in size and barely big enough to stand on while you opened the door.

One day we came home to find a large tarantula spider camped out on the front steps. If you include the size of the legs on this creature, it was as big as a dinner plate. It even looked bigger than that to me. Mom wouldn't get out of the car until Dad used a broom to duel with the denizen of the desert.

Behind our house was a big hill that I named Goat Mountain because wild goats used to graze on the small amount of grass present on the sides of the incline. Goat Mountain was far from a Grand Teton and actually nothing more than a huge pile of dirt. The stink and colored liquid that ran off that hill were so bad that my mom tried to prevent me from climbing on it and enjoying the muck that a young man could easily find. The other side of this man-made pile of debris was an operational copper mine, the source of the green slime and smell that we endured every day. Today I know it must have been an unhealthy environment, and perhaps my folks knew it then, too. But at the time I didn't mind it much because I was having too much fun. I doubt any remnants of that military base still exist, but it would be fun to see the area again.

In 1944 and 1945 it was clear that the war was winding down, but the leadership kept my dad's unit in a training status just in case they needed to deploy. As a result, with little in the way of military duties to perform, the unit spent every day, five days a week, physically working out, eating big meals, and then working out again. When we returned home to Nebraska, three years later, that skinny 135-pound dad was a 220-pound muscle-bound strongman. He continued to look great for a while, but then the easy civilian life changed his physical shape into a 220-pound big overweight man.

My dad's parents lived in a very small house consisting of two bedrooms and one bathroom that did not have a shower. The entire house was probably 750 square feet in size, but it did have an unfinished basement, and that is where my parents and I lived for the first three years after our return from Arizona. The basement where we lived could not have been considered a finished product and was primitive in nature. There were no real walls, and the only structure down there was a coal-burning potbellied stove that was used to heat the upstairs. In the corner of the basement was the ever-present pile of coal that Dad added to the stove several times a day to keep it operating. The downstairs was heated with whatever radiant heat that the furnace gave off. With nothing resembling walls or rooms, wherever you could put a bed, that is where you slept. In the wintertime it could get right chilly, so we moved the mattress closer to the potbelly furnace. And, of course, all five of us—Grandpa, Grandma, Mom, Dad, and me—used the single bathroom and kitchen facilities upstairs. I didn't mind this arrangement, but I imagine that Mom and Dad were continually thinking of ways to improve the conditions.

I'm not sure how the deal transpired, but eventually Grandpa and Grandma moved out and bought an even smaller house about a block away. Somehow, Mom and Dad had managed to become the owners of the original dwelling, so the three of us moved upstairs and took over the whole house. That little house ended up being the home that my folks lived in, raised four kids in, and remained living in until the end of their days.

I had no control over it, but I've always felt bad that I didn't know my brother and sisters better, at least in my younger days. I had no control because I was so much older than Randy, Judy, and Debbie that I was just not around when they were growing up. Randy was six years younger, Judy nine, and Debbie twelve. I was out of high school while they were still in grade school. Randy and I did some fishing together, but most of my recollection of the girls was when I was assigned the task of babysitting.

I was never a really good babysitter because I had a lack of patience. Plus, I didn't want to be stuck home in the first place. One night Debbie managed to take her diaper off, take a dump in her bed, and then stomp around in it, just for fun. By the time I arrived at her bedside, there was quite a mess.

My lack of patience kicked in as I snatched her from the bed and ran to the bathroom. I was not prepared to touch the ugly stuff that covered her feet, so I jammed her feet in the toilet and started a flushing sequence. The water was doing its trick, but Debbie was annoyed. She announced in a very authoritative fashion, "Watch it, big boy." I was not a very good babysitter.

Until I was in high school, my dad was a heavy smoker, usually consuming four or more packs a day. Come to think about it, in those days, every adult I knew was a smoker. As a little kid, Dad would use me as a runner to go buy another pack when he got low, and the closest place for a six-year-old to buy cigarettes was just across the street. Franzen's grocery, a small mom-and-pop store, was only about one hundred yards away, but on the other side of Highway 136. Even though the highway traffic could be heavy at times, it was an easy trek for a kid with a little red wagon. Sounds crazy now, but Dad had trained me well to look for high-speed cars and then to dart to the other side. Harry Franzen was always behind the counter, and he would already have the cigarettes in hand by the time I arrived, so I guess he saw me coming. Dad must have had an account because Harry never asked for money. As soon as the cigarettes were in the wagon, I was off on my return trip over the lined pavement, while on the lookout for big trucks.

Once I was surprised by an oncoming high-speed car, and I panicked. I started to run, and my wagon turned over. I did not stop. I dragged that upside-down wagon to safety on the other side of the street. I had tears in my eyes as I inspected the severe scratches in the wagon paint, but Dad's cigarettes were safe.

Dad abruptly quit smoking when I was a sophomore in high school. I think his reason for quitting was the same reason that I had never smoked. In fact, the most frightened that I had ever been in my young life was on a warm Sunday afternoon in 1957. I was in my basement bedroom, where Dad had recently installed a wall between my bed and the pot-belly stove, creating my own little space. I heard my mother scream, and I raced up the stairs to see Dad lying on his back on the couch. He was unconscious, but his eyes were wide open. Blood was shooting out of his mouth, at least two feet in the air, and there was a terrible noise coming from his throat. I was so scared. I didn't know what to do except just stare.

The ambulance came and took Dad to the Lynch Clinic, which was the small, and only, medical facility in town. I wasn't allowed in the ambulance, so I ran the ten blocks, crying all the way across town, to be at the hospital when Dad arrived.

I was in very good physical condition in those days, but I'm not sure I have ever run that fast before or since. All the time that I was running, I was trying to think about what I would do when I got there. I was convinced that I was losing my father, and I was helpless to prevent the outcome.

Our church was just across the street from the hospital, and as they unloaded Dad, I came up with an idea that I thought might help. I sprinted to Pastor Thompson's house, which was located next door to the church, and banged on the door as loudly as I could. Grover Thompson must have thought I was nuts, because I was wide-eyed and screaming that Dad was dying and he needed to come with me now. I remember crying so hard that the good reverend had trouble understanding my message. I don't know if the pastor coming with me helped Dad, but it sure made me feel a lot better, and Dad didn't die.

The bleeding ulcer was enough to cause Dad to quit cold turkey, and it was also a vivid lesson for his young son. A lesson that all should heed because the thought of not having a dad is frightening. It was good to have that tough old bird back in my face.

Throughout my youth, my mom guarded the home front and taught me to be nice, while Dad pushed me every day to do better at everything that I attempted.

Dad always felt guilty about what he thought were shortcomings in his life, and he was determined that I was not going to make the same mistake of not grabbing at gold-ring opportunities when they presented themselves. He had been presented an opportunity to attend a small college on a football scholarship and he had passed it up. This was a mistake that he was not going to allow me to make. As far as he was concerned, every day of my young life was in preparation for college. He did not suffer my failures very well, and I learned to take heat even when I was successful—no matter how well I did, it was never good enough. By now, it sounds like I didn't like my dad and that he was a terrible person. *Not true.* I now know what he was doing, and I love him for it. Whatever successes that I have had in my life is because of his foot on my ass when I was a kid.

I think it was different when my brother and sisters were growing up, but to me, Dad was like a big, tough brother. He was still young and athletic, and he was always making sure that I was giving 100 percent when it came to sports. Being undersized was not an excuse that he wanted to hear, and I learned that very early on. It seemed like he was everywhere to make sure that I was giving my best effort. He not only attended and critiqued every athletic event that I participated in, he was at every practice session during the week. He didn't get involved in the coaching, but I could see him grimace and make mental notes every time I screwed up. Mom rarely attended games, and I think it was because she was afraid that she would see me get hurt. Unfortunately, due to my undersized frame, that happened a lot.

One example will suffice in illustrating Dad's toughness. During the second quarter of a high school football game, I took a significant blow, and it was clear that my arm was broken because the pain was a bit much. As I sat on the end of the bench with my arm hanging at my side, Dad appeared next to me. He came out of the stands, climbed under the restraining fence, and appeared right next to me. The discussion went something like this: What's wrong?—Dad, my arm's broken—Let me feel it—Feels OK to me. Go tell the coach you are ready to go back in—But, Dad—Go tell the coach—OK.

I did go tell the coach, and he looked at me like I was on drugs, but I went back in. After the game, I couldn't even get undressed because of the pain. The coach took me to the hospital, and the doctor set the arm and put it in a cast. When I got home, Dad said, "What's that?" I explained again that the arm was broken and it needed the cast. His answer was, "OK, but you better be ready to play next Friday," and by the way, "Your play in the third and fourth quarter was poor." And I did play the next Friday! He forced me to do things that on my own terms I would never have tried.

Both of my parents taught me to expect more of myself. My mom's words to me were "Smile, Denny. You have a beautiful smile, and you will make a lot of friends." My dad's advice was "Never give up, and just win." I love them both, for the future they caused me to have.

*Johnny and Vera, my mom and dad, on their wedding day. The photo was taken in front of the farmhouse where Mom's folks lived in Kansas. Interestingly, Mom's parents didn't attend the wedding. I'm told that Grandpa declared that he had too much farmwork to do and couldn't attend.*

*Mom, Dad, and me in front of the old house. Grandpa and Grandma still owned the house when this photo was taken, and we lived in the unfinished basement.*

*This is the house where Mom and Dad raised four children. Note how close the highway is to the side of the house. When trucks drove by, the whole house shook. The house used to have a porch with a roof that went across the entire front. The small porch offered little protection for my bicycle during blowing snowstorms.*

*Mom and her twin sister, Vesta. It was hard to tell them apart, and they loved to wear the same clothes to confuse people. My mom is on the left, I think.*

*My paternal grandparents, Almon and Mary. Grandpa was a great carpenter, but he lost several fingers to wayward power tools. Grandpa smoked cigarettes and died when he was seventy-six. Grandma lived to be 101. Neither had ever had a drink of alcohol.*

*They were both very frugal. I once borrowed twelve dollars from them to help me buy a car. They tracked my payments, dollar by dollar, in a little book that they kept near their bed.*

*Grandma drove a stick-shift Ford Fairlane well into her nineties. She couldn't see over the steering wheel, so she looked through it. Every Sunday she would travel around town to pick up some younger ladies on their way to church. The younger ladies were in their late eighties.*

*Dad and two buddies goofing off in Bisbee, Arizona, where we lived during his first duty station.*

*A proud soldier getting ready to report for duty. Note the small house across the street. Ours was even smaller.*

*Mad Dog in his letter sweater. Hard to believe that at 135 pounds, Dad was thought to be the meanest guy on the team. The only undefeated team that our hometown high school ever had was in Dad's senior year.*

*Sisters Debbie and Judy with brother Randy. The four of us are dressed in our Sunday finest.*

When the sisters came along, Dad put up a thin wall in the unfinished basement so Randy and I could have our own room. It was the first time that there had ever been any separation from the coal-burning furnace.

*During World War II, everyone had to have a ration card, even a two-year-old.*

*Dad outside one of the Army Air Corps offices in Bisbee. The buildings were all very flimsy, and our house didn't look much different.*

*There were a lot of stray animals in the Arizona desert, and
I decided to rescue this cute pup. Mom decided otherwise,
saying that the house was not big enough for the three of us
plus a dog.*

*A mean desperado sitting on the side of Goat Mountain.*
*Our house was just in front of me, and on the other side of*
*the hill was a copper mine. The runoff from the mine was*
*green and stinky, but fun to play in.*

*A friend and I take a little afternoon bike ride in the Arizona desert.*

*Dad always needed help getting his dirty uniforms into the house. It was my job to come to the rescue. I'm sitting on our front porch.*

*Dad and I staying cool in the hot Arizona sun.*

*Nothing like a little hot tub time after a hard day's work.*

*Brother Randy and I getting ready for the season.*

## CHAPTER 2

## The Farm

———————

Some of my first and fondest memories of childhood involved the farm. We didn't live on a farm, but my maternal grandparents did, and I spent a lot of time in rural Kansas. Grandpa and Grandma only lived about twenty miles from our house in Fairbury, but in those days it seemed like an all-day journey just to get there. The roads leading to the homestead were not the wonderful asphalt or concrete type you see today but just good-old country dirt. If there was any kind of rain or snow, the roads could become impassable because the wheels of the car would sink into the soil, right up to the axle. When it snowed, the drifts across the road could be five or six feet deep, and there were few snow plows to aid in removal. I can remember many times when we would get within about a half mile of the house and Grandpa would have to meet us with the tractor to either pull the car the rest of the way or just transfer everyone for a tractor ride. I'm sure it didn't help that we were driving 1930-vintage cars.

The farm itself was typical of a family-owned endeavor in those days. If a farmer owned a quarter section, or 160 acres of land, he could feed his family and, in a good year, make a living. Anything much bigger than that would have been a chore to farm by a single farmer. Individual farm families just didn't have the manpower or the machinery that would have been needed to plant and harvest that much land. As I recall, Grandpa had about a quarter section, but my uncle helped him maintain the land, and not all of it was in crops. There was some pasture land for the few head of cattle that he raised, and of course there was the fallow, or unfarmed, land that was waiting for next year's planting.

The farm had been in the family for a long time, so additions had been made to the main house over the years. From the outside, the house looked like a two-story building, but the upper floor was more like an attic, and it was full of junk. I'm sure that at one time the upstairs had been a living space, but not during my lifetime. I was on that upper floor a couple of times, under the supervision of an adult. But to my knowledge, people didn't go up there very often. I wonder why? That upstairs area of the house looked dangerous to me. I guess I should have asked.

Neither the house nor the outbuildings were well maintained, and everything looked like it could use a good paint job. There were bigger priorities than cosmetic building upkeep for farmers, and most of them had to do with survival. Years later, when the farm was abandoned, I was saddened to see the house start to cave in. There was no need for demolition; the house just collapsed.

It seemed to me that Grandpa had a lot of buildings, and I liked that because it gave me many places to play. About fifty yards straight across from the house was the main barn that housed a hay mow, full bales of hay used to feed the cattle. This same barn was where the milk cows and hogs were kept at night. About halfway between the house and the barn was the root cellar. The root cellar was nothing more than a hole in the yard, with stairs leading down into a dirt cave. The cave contained many old wooden shelves that were loaded with food items that would get us through the winter. Freshly canned fruits and vegetables, as well as potatoes, carrots, and onions were always present.

The entrance to the root cellar was covered with an old wooden door that Grandpa had removed from a shed. The root cellar also played a secondary role in farm life because it was the place we would run to when there was a tornado in the area. Many times I can remember being swept off my feet by a running Grandma as we headed to the safety of that musty old hole in the ground.

To the left of the house was a building that was called the wash house because it contained an ancient-looking washing machine that was operated by a small gasoline motor. I'm pretty sure that the motor had previously been removed from some other unknown device.

When the motor was running, it made so much noise and heavy smoke and fumes that you didn't want this thing close to the house. Like everything else on the farm, the rest of the wash house was full of junk. I didn't play there much because I found the place to be kind of creepy. My recollection is that the washer didn't work much of the time because I normally saw my grandmother doing the laundry by hand with a scrub board and a big tub.

A little farther out from the wash house was the corncrib, which contained the eared corn that would be necessary for feeding the livestock through the winter. This building also had a covered area where the Farmall tractor was kept when not in use. That tractor was special to Grandpa because it was expensive, and until he got it, he had farmed with mules. The corncrib was fun to play in because there were always rats and mice that you could attempt to catch. Except for the pink baby mice, which there was a host of, I didn't have much luck as a hunter. Probably just as well!

A few hundred yards beyond the main barn was another cattle barn, which we referred to as the new barn. Being constructed in the 1930s gave it the distinction of being new—clearly much newer than the old barn. The new barn didn't last very long and was destined to become a fatality of Kansas weather. One very hot summer afternoon my play was interrupted by a screaming old lady in a calico dress as she charged across the farmyard. Grandma scooped me up, and we disappeared into the root cellar as the wind started to kick up. I wasn't old enough to understand true fear, but when Grandma got excited, I knew it was time to listen. As we peered through a crack in the old wooden door, the sky turned black, the clouds billowed and rolled, and it sounded like we were standing next to a locomotive. Suddenly, a funnel cloud dropped from the roiling sky and started moving from west to east across the pasture.

It seemed to bounce and skip as it approached the place that we were hiding. When it would hit the ground out in the pasture, dirt and debris would fly and windmills would disappear. When it was off the ground, things looked to be untouched. Unfortunately, the tornado chose to execute a direct hit on the new barn, and as we watched, the barn appeared to raise right off its foundation in one piece, momentarily shake, and then disintegrate. Later in life, I would see the movie *The Wizard of Oz* and remark that animals flying through the sky was exactly what I had seen on that scary Kansas afternoon. When the funnel cloud was done with the new barn, it rose up and jumped right over the old barn before touching down right where we were hiding. The old wooden door over our heads withstood the wind, and then the funnel cloud skipped right over the top of the house. Not even a house shingle was harmed as we watched the funnel proceed to the east to cause more damage in Republic County, Kansas. We spent the better part of that summer picking up barn lumber and removing nails so that animals didn't step on them. Unfortunately, my normal summer practice was not to wear shoes, so when I stepped on a nail, we made a quick trip to the country doctor for a tetanus shot.

There were various other silos and granaries on the premises, but the most important remaining edifice was the outhouse. This important building, set off to the side of the main house, was about a fifty-yard dash in distance. You did not want to have a call of nature during a cold, snowy, and windy night. Toilet paper was something that was never found on the farm, but there was always an abundant supply of Spiegel, Sears, or Montgomery Ward catalogs available for reading and eventual handiwork. Additionally, Grandpa always had a bushel of corn cobs in the corner of the privy. He claimed that they did a more thorough job of cleanup. If I had an urgent call of nature when out in the field with him, he required me to use the nearest cob that I could find. I can't tell you that it was a pleasant experience, but I can tell you that it was effective.

Indoor plumbing did not appear at Grandma and Grandpa's place until I was well into my teenage years. After all bodily function activities were moved indoors, the garden was expanded to cover the land where the old outhouse had stood for years. The vegetable crops that were planted in that garden did exceedingly well.

We did have a telephone in the house, and it looked like the ones you see in the Smithsonian. A large wooden box with a crank on the side, a speaking horn on the front, and a receiver hanging from a cord that you held to your ear during a call. When you wanted to make a call, you cranked the telephone and a lady named May, who was in a town named Mahaska about a mile away, would answer. You would tell May who you wanted to call, and she would move plug cables around on a big vertical board and magically connect you—at least sometimes. The phone system itself was a party line on steroids because everyone in the county was on the same system. When your phone rang, every phone in the county rang, and my guess is that almost all of those phones were picked up and your neighbors listened to every word. Each home on the system had its own distinct ring. Grandpa's was one long and two short, but nobody paid attention to privacy, and there were no secrets in rural Kansas.

Learning to live without electricity was another of those experiences that makes you appreciate the luxury of today's world. Farmers work hard, very hard, but they usually make sure that the majority of their chores are complete by the time the sun goes down. That means around nine p.m. in the summertime. After that, everything must be accomplished by the light of a kerosene lantern. A kerosene lantern gives off a sufficient amount of eerie light, but it must be moved around as you work, and this can be a nuisance. Not to mention that the open flame, even with a lantern globe, can be a fire hazard. Because there were so many lanterns around the house, I can still smell the dirty aroma of burning kerosene oil.

My kids always ask what we did for entertainment after the daily farm work was done. Most farmers are so tired that just going to bed is all they have on their minds. However, Grandpa loved baseball, and the St. Louis Cardinals in particular. Not sure how he knew when the Cardinals were playing because there were no newspapers to advertise it, but he had a sense. So, each evening when there was a game being played, he would hope that the atmospherics were in place so that he could listen to the game on the St. Louis radio station that was positioned about three hundred miles away. If there were too many clouds or rainstorms, there was no chance of getting a signal from that distance.

The big old tube-type radio sat by the potbelly stove in the living room, and it was no normal-looking contraption. It was huge by today's standards, being about two feet wide and three feet tall. But the most interesting part of the setup was how Grandpa powered the device. He stacked twelve to fifteen car batteries against the wall, behind the stove. He connected them in parallel, then to the radio, and presto, we were listening to Stan Musial hit home runs. I have often wondered how Grandpa kept those batteries charged up. Sometimes on a summer evening Grandpa would decide that it was time to relax by reducing the herd of rats that were always present on the farm. In addition to living in the corncrib, the rats would burrow holes and long tunnels in the yard between the house and the barn. Hunting the rats was fun for me because I not only got to watch, I got to participate. We would rig up a long water hose from the hand pump at the main well that was next to the house and then run the hose out to the middle of the yard. My mother would pump like crazy on the hand crank, in order to deliver the water down the hose, while I would direct the nozzle of the hose into one of the rat holes, trying to flush the vermin out. Grandpa would sit in his rocker on the porch, pointing and directing to which holes I should attend, while he awaited the coming action. When the associated tunnel was full, you could expect water to start spurting out of another hole about twenty feet away. Shortly thereafter, a wet rat would stick his head up and a shot would be fired. Grandpa would have his first kill of the evening, and I would move on to the next hole. Grandpa was a very good shot.

When Grandpa really got bored, he and I would take a tractor ride down to the railroad crossing about a mile south of the house. He knew that I loved to watch the Gandy Dancers do their work. The Gandy Dancers were mostly black, and they were workers who went up and down the rails looking for places that needed repair. My favorite part of their job was watching them operate the hand pump cart that they traveled on. The Dancers always seemed happy to see us, and they let me walk around the jobsite and inspect their tools. As they traveled down the rails, you could hear them singing in the distance.

Living on a farm meant that there were no other kids to play with. My cousins would come by from time to time, but I was mostly on my own when it came to entertaining myself. As a result, I had several imaginary friends who kept me company. The closest farms were about a mile or so away, and I can remember when we would pass their houses, Grandpa would say, "That is where the Duncans live," or "That is where the Petersons live." I didn't know who those people were, but I assumed that they must be good folks, and perhaps they had kids. Also, being very young, I couldn't pronounce their names properly. Therefore, I invented my two closest imaginary companions, who lived at those two farmhouses, and their names were Truncan and Meterson. The three of us spent a lot of time together.

There was one week out of every year that I was not allowed to play outside the house. That was the week that the Gypsies showed up and camped about a mile south. Grandpa said they were like clockwork every year as they rolled in on their colorful covered wagons. I don't know where they came from or where they went, but during that week, Grandpa was on alert. I was told that Gypsies stole children and that I was a prime target. I believed the adults, and I stayed indoors. Grandpa, on the other hand, spent the week on the porch with a loaded ten-gauge shotgun. Grandpa was an expert in watching Gypsy movements, and he knew when they were in the henhouse stealing chickens. He always said that as long as they only stole one or two, he wouldn't shoot. Any more than that, and there was going to be flaming trouble. Grandpa's system must have worked because I didn't get stolen and I never heard that gun go off.

I never knew my grandfather to drink alcohol, but I'm sure he did. The only time I saw liquor at the farm was at Christmas and Thanksgiving. On those holidays, a big bottle of Mogen David wine would show up on the table and the adults would pretend to drink "just a little."

Grandpa did love his chewing tobacco, and he was never without chaw in his mouth. His favorite brand was Red Man, and I was always happy when he opened a new pouch. Each new pouch of Red Man came with a picture of a famous Indian chief, similar to baseball trading cards but much bigger. Each time Grandpa opened a new batch, my Indian card collection got bigger.

My great-grandmother, Grandma Bentley, lived with us until she passed away. She was very old, even when I was little, so my grandmother would ask me to help entertain her as she rocked in her chair and observed the farmyard from her window. I guess it was like a job for me, but when there is no one else to play with, you make the most of it. Grandma Bentley either had an eyesight problem or she was a little touched because she would argue with me about what we were seeing in the farmyard. One day she said, "Look at that dog, it seems to be walking funny." I looked, and then I looked again, before exclaiming, "That is not a dog, it's a chicken." Grandma Bentley and I argued a lot.

When Grandma Bentley died, they laid her out, in a box, in the back room of the house. There was not much embalming of dead bodies in those days, so it was important to get her in the ground as soon as possible. All the neighbors came to say good-bye to Grandma Bentley, so while they ate the food that everyone brought, we kids played around and under the table that Grandma occupied. Seemed very natural. When most of the food was gone, they put Grandma Bentley on a wagon bed, and we went off to the cemetery. Even though there was a neat player piano and an old wind-up Victrola in the back room, I never did like to play in there anymore. Couldn't help thinking of Grandma Bentley.

When it was time to go to bed, some major decisions needed to be made. Did I really need to make the trek to the outhouse or could I hold it all night? It could be a painful journey if I woke up at two o'clock in the morning and had to make a freezing trip to the privy. Because of that, I usually chose to go to the privy before bed, but I would only go halfway to the outhouse before I stopped and just peed on the ground. I suspect that Grandma knew.

During the winter months, with no electricity or heat other than the potbelly stove, just getting to bed was an adventure. Using the cob-burning stove in the kitchen, Grandma would heat up the anvil part of a clothes iron for each of us. Once heated up, the hot anvil would be wrapped in a towel, which we would then carry to the bedroom. Once in the bedroom, we would put the towel-wrapped iron under the covers at the foot of the bed. The warmth would last long enough for you to get to sleep, and then for the rest of the night you were on your own body heat. I'm sure it was a strange sight, seeing each of us headed down the hall carrying a heavy hot towel and a kerosene lantern. The shadows that were cast and danced on the walls looked like ghosts. The next morning, you started farm life all over again.

It seemed like there was an endless list of chores that required completion twice a day, and when they were complete, it was time to do them again.

I was not fond of looking after the chickens. The coops where the chickens were housed were closed in and stifling, with no openings for air flow. If you had any openings in the coops that were bigger than a crack, the weasels would get in and eat the chickens. The smell of chicken manure was also very distinct, and it was at least three inches deep, slippery, and unpleasant.

Once the chicken feed had been put out, it was time to gather the eggs, and this could be a dangerous task for a little kid. The setting hens seemed to always be sitting on the very eggs that I wanted to gather. Grandma used the technique of roughly reaching under the hen, while pushing up on the breast and pulling the eggs from beneath. Seemed to work for her, but when I did it, the hen would reach down and peck me on the hand. I would get the egg and a bloody hand, while the next hen would wait her turn to attack me. I learned to cuss while gathering eggs.

The fenced-in portion of the farmyard, where the animals were loose, seemed to always be wet. Wet is not descriptive enough because the barnyard was usually one- to two-feet deep in mud and manure. It doesn't sound very good, but the hogs loved it, and that is where they spent most of their time, lying around in the muck. I watched from a distance when the hogs were being slopped because Grandpa was afraid that I might not survive a head-on collision with a three-hundred-pound sow. Watching was fine with me. The pigs ate from a specially concocted menu that was called "mash," and they would stampede to the trough when Grandpa called "Soooey." Not sure what soooey meant, but the pigs understood. Mash was brewed in a fifty-five-gallon wood barrel, and the ingredients were water, barley, shelled corn, and wheat. After sitting in the barrel for three to four days, the grains would become soft, and the soupy mash was ready to be consumed. There were four to five barrels of mash working all the time, but you had to be careful not to let the mash work more than three to four days. If you let the mixture work too long, it would start to ferment, and then you had the problem of inebriated pork wandering around the barnyard, oinking in an incoherent fashion. When the roosters would get into an overripe barrel, they would chase the hens.

You need strong hands if you are going to milk cows, and you were presented with an opportunity to prove your strength, twice a day. The milk cows would be driven into the barn and, without much direction, each one knew exactly which stall she should stand in. Grandma did the milking, and she had the routine down to a science. Equipped with her three-legged milk stool, a large galvanized bucket, and a set of "cow kickers," she would enter each stall while uttering her first command, "Whoa, bossy." That meant *stand still*, and the cows did because they were happy to see her. Grandma said that if cows don't get milked properly twice a day, it can be very painful for the cow, and the cow will eventually go dry or stop giving milk. I believed her. The cow kickers looked like a huge set of handcuffs with a strong chain between them. These cuffs were put on the hind legs of the cow so that the cow couldn't kick the milker while the evolution was in progress. Cows hate flies, and they will kick if bitten.

As soon as Grandma was perched on her stool, the numerous farm cats would arrive for their twice-daily take of the white gold. There was always a dozen or so cats living in the farmyard, and they knew exactly where to sit, if they were to get their share. As a side note, too many cats and dogs on a farm can be a nuisance. Grandpa was intolerant of this situation and maintained a loaded .22-caliber rifle for use every six to eight months, but I digress. The cats would sit to the side of Grandma, in a perfect line, while she would commence the work of milking the cow. Every sixth or seventh pull of the tit, she would direct the flow stream toward the cats' mouths and make sure the flow went down the full length of waiting felines. When the flow was going to the bucket, the cat's mouths were closed, but when they sensed it was their turn, all of the mouths would open in unison as the flow began. This well-choreographed theater would have made it big with a lot of hits on Facebook.

Corn and corn cobs were a necessity for everyday events on the farm, and one of my unique chores was to ensure a steady supply of shelled corn and cobs. The separating of the corn from the cob was just what a young man needed to build up his muscles and to ensure his usefulness around the farm. The equipment used in shelling corn, interestingly known as the "sheller," was about five feet tall and was made up of a series of gears that were turned by a hand crank.

As you fed the corn into the gears, you turned the crank, and the teeth of the mechanism ripped the kernels from the cob and then dumped the cob to the side. Meanwhile, the shelled corn would exit a spout and into a bucket that was strategically placed. If you didn't keep a good rhythm and constant turning action on the crank, the corn would get hung up in the gears, and you would grind to a screeching halt. Delays like this were not good and brought your usefulness as a good worker into question. At least that is what Grandpa used to say.

The corn was always needed in large supply for the feeding of the livestock, but the cobs were equally important. In the Midwest there is a limited supply of wood that can be used in fireplaces or cookstoves, so corn cobs were the next best fuel supply. Come to think of it, I cannot recall ever seeing wood being used as a fuel. Grandma had a large basket next to the iron kitchen stove that I kept full of cobs. As she cooked, she would give me the order when it was time to throw a few more cobs into the firebox. That old iron stove not only provided some good meals, the heat it gave off would warm half the house. The other half of the house was heated in the evening by burning cobs in the living room potbelly stove. And, as previously discussed, if Grandpa's outhouse basket was not full of cobs, you could hear him bellow all the way to the other side of the farm.

There was a menagerie of animals on the farm and many hungry mouths to feed. In the case of hogs, cattle, and chickens, the quantity of animals could be large. However, Grandma always had a couple of individual creatures she was fattening up for special occasions. She made sure that the two or three turkeys got a little extra food in November. I was never fond of the one or two geese that roamed the farmyard because I had determined that they were the meanest animals on earth. I thought I was pretty fast, but if the geese decided you were in their territory, they would chase you, and they were really fast. When they hit their stride, with their wings flapping and their heads bobbing, they emanated a terrible hiss from snapping bills. If someone tells you that geese don't bite, they are lying. I enjoyed it when Christmas came and went because the geese disappeared.

My favorite animals were Grandpa's mules and Smokey, the only horse on the farm. Smokey was never used as a beast of burden or as a work animal. He just ate, got fat, and was a joy for me and the other grandchildren to ride. It is hard for me to visualize how big a horse he was, but to a little kid he seemed huge, so I am thankful that he was so gentle. I always rode bareback because we didn't own a saddle. When I sat on Smokey's back, my legs would stick straight out sideways from my body because of his girth. Dressed up in a cowboy outfit, toting a shiny cap pistol, and sitting astride my steed, Smokey, I imagined myself as a real cowpoke.

The reason that I liked the mules was because they were probably the most useful animals on the place, and I loved the way they would get under Grandpa's skin. Before a tractor was purchased, the mules were the primary means of making things happen, including working the crops and pulling wagons around the farm. Some days you needed the mules to move grain or hog slop. On other days, there was the nasty job of scooping manure out of the henhouse and into the mule-drawn manure spreader, then discharging the contents of the load into a waiting field as fertilizer. I didn't like riding with Grandpa on the manure spreader because the manure did not always go where intended. There were other field and crop activities that I did enjoy, and Grandpa made sure I was as comfortable as a little kid could be on a hot, dusty summer afternoon. There was usually only one seat on most of the field equipment, like the plow, the planter, and the disc. Grandpa fixed the problem by welding a second seat next to him so he and I could have some quality time while in the field.

It was during these memorable days alone with Grandpa in the field that I had to remember not to giggle out loud as I witnessed the interaction of man and beast. My uncle had some Shetland ponies that he claimed were the orneriest animals alive, but those ponies had nothing on Grandpa's mules.

I'm sure that the mules knew they were overworked, and at times they would just stop. Right in the middle of the field, they would both come to a complete halt and just stand there while Grandpa would yell at them, snap the reins, and then yell some more. But those mules would not move. Grandpa's next maneuver was to jump off the seat, run around in front of the mules, and scream obscenities in their faces. I mean, he would get forehead to forehead with the beasts and bellow, as I'm holding back a belly full of laughter. The animals wouldn't move, and I knew what was coming next because Grandpa would be headed for the toolbox. Out would come a big hammer, and he would show up in front of the mules again. By this time the old farmer was enraged by the animals' insubordination, and he was waving the hammer in front of their faces and threatening them with a mighty blow if they didn't get back to work.

Grandpa was never a big man, just a little over five feet, four inches tall. However, he was extremely athletic-looking, wiry and strong. When Grandpa ate, he ate like he was feeding a three-hundred-pound man, so those mules knew that when Grandpa got angry, there was going to be some pain involved.

When he waved that hammer in front of their eyes, they knew he was serious. When he would yell, "Move!" and nothing happened—and it normally didn't—he would whack them both between the eyes. He would then run around, jump back into his seat, and the mules would go back to work. I didn't like the whacking much, but it was fun to see the old man get excited, and the remedy seemed to work. I often wondered if it was the whacking that made the mules move or that they had finally rested long enough. I sensed that Grandpa truly loved those mules because he spoke highly of them when they were not within earshot.

The fall season was a very busy time on the farm because preparations needed to be made for surviving the coming winter months. Grandma's garden was one of the most productive pieces of property on the entire farm, so we had fresh vegetables and fruits throughout the summer. However, the end-of-the-season harvest was also extremely important. The potato patch alone covered an area of about two acres, so when the time came, there was a lot of digging to be done. In addition to the potatoes, carrots and onions would be packed into individual gunnysacks, and the sacks would be loaded onto the shelves in the root locker. Grandma, Mom, and the other women would spend days in the kitchen, going through the laborious task of canning fruits and vegetables that were then placed on their respective shelves in the underground cornucopia.

Meanwhile, Grandpa and my uncle were in charge of gathering the meat supply for the winter. This meant it was time to butcher a hog and a steer. For me, this was an important learning process because throughout the year I had given names to some of the animals that were about to go under the knife. My instructions from Grandpa were to "Be tough" and "This is the way of the world." Once that I understood those rules, I was ready to help. Grandpa's .22-caliber rifle came into play again during the butchering process. After the designated animal was led to the covered area between the corncribs, the animal was dispatched and its hind legs were tied together. The animal was then hoisted up by a rope and a large pulley that was attached to the roof. Once in a vertical position, the animal was skinned, and then the actual cutting of various steaks and pork chops began. Some portions of butchered meat were set aside, and I was put to work running the meat through a hand-operated grinder, turning it into hamburger. It always amazed me that Grandpa knew how to butcher the animal such that the steaks and chops came from the right place on the carcass. I guess that just comes with being a farmer all your life. There were many sharp knives lying around during this process, so I needed to keep a good distance, but there was some fun to be had. Grandpa would lop off the pig's curly tail, give it to me, and I'd chase Mom around the yard with the fuzzy thing.

The women would package the meat in white butcher paper, label the contents, and stack the finished product in the back of the Model A Ford. The next step was to get the packaged meat to a freezer, and that meant driving the mile to Mahaska, where at least one building had electricity.

That building was known as the Locker, and I think every family within twenty miles of Mahaska relied on the Locker to preserve their meats after the butchering process. The inside of the Locker building was like the inside of a room-sized walk-in freezer, and each family had a designated drawer inside the freezer room. The drawers were about three feet wide, two feet tall, five feet deep, and they could hold all the packages that we delivered. During the year, even during bad weather, all we needed to do was take the tractor, go to Mahaska and get some meat from the family drawer. Come to think of it, I believe that the other part of the Locker building is where May, the telephone operator, resided, so that building was super important.

My dad had a private pilot's license, which I think he received by using the GI Bill after the war. There is no other way that he could have afforded flying lessons on his salary. Once every month or so we would go to the Fairbury airport and rent a Piper Cub so Dad could maintain his proficiency. These very small aircraft had two seats, the pilot in front and a small seat behind. Dad would stack up parachute bags on the second seat so that I could see out the window while we soared at two thousand to three thousand feet above the countryside. By today's standards the Pipers were not the safest-looking aircraft because they were constructed mostly of cloth and wood. Oh, there was probably a little amount of metal in the fuselage, but not much. I admit that at times I was a little scared, but Dad loved the airborne time, and you could see the happiness in his eyes every time we went aloft. I know he regretted that he was an airplane mechanic and hadn't gotten to be a pilot during the war.

I mention Dad's pilot license because once a year, in the fall, Dad would plan his proficiency flight to coincide with a visit to the farm. Mom would join us during those flights, and I would sit on her lap in the second seat. The flight was only twenty miles long, but we planned for it like it was a major cross-country jaunt. Part of the planning was arranging for a place to land at the farm. The half-mile-long field, just south of the house, was normally planted with alfalfa or left to pasture, so that was the favored landing strip. Grandpa would get the mower out and cut a passable landing strip in the field, and we would come swooping out of the sky, taxiing right up to the farmhouse. After a day of family interaction, it was time to return to Fairbury, and that is when things got a little scary. You never left my grandparents' house without a lot of things that you didn't come with. The small compartment behind the second seat in the plane would be jammed with gunnysacks full of potatoes, squash, onions, cartons of eggs, and packages of meat, until nothing more would fit. We would say our good-byes, climb into our assigned positions, and taxi to the very far end of the field. The sixty-five-horsepower engine of that little beast would roar as Dad pushed the throttle all the way to the panel. The plane would pick up speed nicely, and Dad would be pulling back on the stick as hard as he could in an effort to get the craft to escape the grasp of gravity. However, by the time we had covered three-quarters of the homemade runway, it was clear that the plane was too heavy, and we would not make it. We would taxi back to the house, and after a lot of discussion, we would unload the vittles until we thought we had reached a weight that the little airplane could handle. After two or three of these attempts, and trips to the house for load correction, the plane would finally lift off, just in time to clear the barbed-wire fence at the end of the field. There would be three voices in the plane cheering as we cleared Grandpa and Grandma's heads by about ten feet, en route home with the loot. There didn't seem to be many aircraft rules back then, but my guess is that if there were, we broke a lot them.

Impressions are everything when you are young and learning the ways of the world. Life on the farm taught me that it takes hard work to make it, and maybe some of the hardest workers in the world are the family farmers. No matter where I went or what I did in later life, there were challenges that caused me to reflect on what I had learned throughout my childhood. Many times when I was searching for answers, I would just stop and think to myself, "What would Grandpa and Grandma do?" I usually came up with the right answer.

*Leslie and Bertha Cossaart, my maternal grandparents and hardworking dryland Kansas farmers. Grandpa could fix anything, and Grandma saved me from several torna-does. I'm told that I look a lot like Grandpa, and that is fine with me.*

*It always seemed like Grandpa was working so hard; however, Grandma took great pride in pushing him even harder. What a team.*

*A very young Denny, sitting on the old Case tractor. The corncrib is in the background.*

*Smokey, the greatest horse that ever lived. No reins or saddle were necessary. I would just climb on and pretend I was a Wild West cowboy.*

*Feeling pretty special in some new threads. The hat set off the entire ensemble.*

*Coveralls were my normal work, and play, clothes. I needed plenty of body protection while playing all day in the dirt. Grandpa always wore coveralls, and I wanted to look just like him.*

*Taking a ride around the farmyard. The building behind me is what we called the old barn. The area between me and the barn is where we would flush rats out of the ground for Grandpa to shoot.*

*The three of us in front of Grandpa and Grandma's Kansas farmhouse. This was taken just before Dad left for Arizona. Mom and I stayed on the farm for a while before following him south. The little porch behind the car is where Grandpa sat while shooting rats.*

*Four generations—my great-grandmother Bentley on the left, and my grandmother Bertha on the right, with Mom and me. For a while, we all lived together in a rustic Kansas farmhouse. As I got a little older, it was my job to babysit my great-grandmother, and she would, at times, say some very strange things.*

*The old farmstead. This photo was taken before my time, but things had not changed that much. Behind the house is the old barn on the right and the corncrib on the left. The big closed door on the left side of the corncrib is where we would hang animals while we were butchering. Note the well by the house—this is where Mom would pump water while I carried the hose to flush out the rats. The wash house was just outside of the photo to the left.*

*The running board of the old Ford Model A made a perfect seat while enjoying a cold beverage.*

## CHAPTER 3

## Colene

———————

I'm not sure when it happens to most young boys, but for me kindergarten was the year of my first romance. I know it must sound strange, but even at five years old I knew that girls were special and that one of the challenges for a young male was to capture the smiles of the prettiest girl in the class. At this point, smiles were good enough. The attempt at other booty would come later.

My kindergarten classroom was probably like every other kindergarten classroom in the Midwest: a very small room with miniature desks, a large teacher's table, and, of course, lots and lots of chalkboard all around the room. The wall in the back of the room was covered with small cubicles, about twelve inches square. Each student had his or her own cubicle to store books and other school items. Additionally in the cubicle we stored the small rugs that we would rest on after playtime.

I did not really like going to the board to solve problems because the teacher could easily determine that I didn't know what I was doing. Besides being scolded by the teacher, my classmates then would have a good laugh at my expense.

Ms. Isabel Shoebotham was her name, and she had been teaching kindergarten in the same classroom for more years than most people can remember. She was perfectly typecast as a kindergarten teacher. She was tall and skinny with the walking characteristics of a big bird, but in an elegant way. Her hair was always pulled back and rolled up in a bun. I remember her long, thin, and bony fingers, which were pointed at me on many occasions. She had never been married, and as a result her whole life was dedicated to the education of the youth of Fairbury, Nebraska. The fact of the matter is that she had taught my father and every other person still living in my small town. The burden that this fact hoisted on me was enormous. If I did not behave, she knew exactly where my parents could be found, at any minute of the day. If that call went out to my parents, it was more than a simple report about my ill behavior. Ms. Isabel would also take the opportunity to lecture my father about how his son was just as academically challenged, and as unteachable, as he had been years ago. This was a call that I did want to happen because my father could be a very tough customer when I got home. He loved Ms. Isabelle, but he did not want to be lectured by her.

In those days kindergarten was a full-day struggle. None of this partial-day stuff for the young citizens of Central Ward. You started at eight in the morning and finished at four in the afternoon, and sick days were not tolerated. On top of a midafternoon playtime and a delicious lunch of milk, crackers, and fruit, there was also one other cherished daily event—nap time.

Nap time was deemed necessary by the school board because a full day of academics and exercise could wear out a young body. But for me the logistics of nap time added to the excitement of the hunt because nap time was when Colene came into my life.

On the first day of kindergarten each student was issued a small rug; small by adult standards, but large enough so that a five-year-old could comfortably stretch out on it. As I recall, these rugs looked very similar in weaving and colorful design as

I would later see on ponchos in Tijuana. My guess is that these same rugs had been used by my father and his classmates because they were well-worn. A deep inhalation would also reveal that the rugs had an ancient odor. However, now they were ours, and we loved them, so it was our job to make sure they were taken care of. We were required to carefully roll them up when not in use and stow them on a shelf next to our books and other school supplies. This we dutifully did. It was a simple task to roll the rugs out on the floor when it was time for a nap.

When Ms. Isabel issued the order to prepare for nap time, I would snatch my rug from the shelf and muscle my way to a position next to Colene. When the follow-on order to lie down on the floor came— there I was, lying next to the prettiest girl in the class—Colene. This was the best part of the day.

Colene was well developed for a five-year-old. By that I mean she was bigger and much taller than most of the boys. A lot taller than me. I didn't care because she had the most beautiful red hair that I had ever seen. Actually, I had never seen red hair before, but I knew it was beautiful, and it made me feel good just looking at it. Ms. Isabel had declared that no one was allowed to touch anyone else during nap time, so I just laid there and watched that red hair while Colene napped. I suspect that in today's world

I'd be on my way to the principal's office right now for being weird.

Earlier I mentioned that nap time was a daily logistical challenge. I'm sure the reader has determined that getting into the proper position to rest next to Colene was an easy matter. It was not. It took great ingenuity and tenacity and caused enormous stress because I was always challenged by my best friend, Bob.

You see, Bob also had an eye for red hair, and he was very competitive when it came to nap time. Bob was a lot bigger than me, so I relied on speed and stealth when Ms. Isabel announced nap time. Actually, I can't think of one person—boy or girl—in my class who wasn't bigger than me. Maybe it was just wishful thinking, but Coleen seemed much happier when I won the contest, but Bob didn't seem to be as happy.

Even though Colene and I continued in school together for many years, we never dated, but we remained close friends. However, every once in a while, I would see that twinkle in her eye that told me that I was always her favorite. My last teenage memory of her happened on a New Year's Eve during high school, just prior to her moving away from town.

Some of the parents had sponsored a party to ensure that we teenagers would not go out and get in trouble while celebrating the New Year. The party was one of those gatherings that you would expect when a parent did the planning. A little dancing, some punch and cookies, snacks, and, of course, fun games. Without the proper adult supervision throughout the evening, there also was some harmless backroom necking.

Somehow, a bottle of champagne suddenly appeared on the scene. Being very quick and stealthy, I declared that a toast was in order and we needed to do it before the chaperones reappeared. I remember thinking how cool I was. With that, I seized Colene's shoe, a high heel as I recall, poured bubbly into it, and promptly drank to her good health. To this day I have no idea why I would do such a thing, but I think she was impressed.

Colene moved away during the early years of our high school days, but she always stayed in touch with the class. She even returned on many occasions to enjoy the reunions. Seems that she achieved her childhood dream of becoming a dancer in Las Vegas, married a captain of industry, and lived happily ever after.

Kindergarten was a very good year—I always loved that red hair.

*The Central Ward kindergarten class of 1947. I'm the little guy on the far left in the front row. Colene is on the far left in the second row. Seems that I got close to her for photos also. Bob is the tall guy in the back, a long way from Colene. Perhaps I planned it that way.*

*Proof that I passed kindergarten. And more importantly, I gained three pounds during the year.*

## CHAPTER 4

## Best Friends

——————

Everybody should have a friend whom they have known their entire life. As I write this manifesto, it has been almost seventy years since I first met my friend Bob, and his name will show up in many of the succeeding chapters. At four years of age, we started kindergarten together. Over the many years that passed, we competed in athletics, academics, and for girlfriends. Actually, we only competed for the fairer sex and in athletics because it would not have been a fair fight if I had tried to keep up with Bob's academic capabilities. Bob was very smart and worked diligently in school, while I was lazy and did not pay enough attention to the grading system.

In pre-computer days, the key to all knowledge was the *Encyclopedia Britannica*, a multivolume compilation of everything you can now get with the push of a single computer button. It took tenacity and time to look up a single fact, and as a young man in a hurry to grow up, I had neither. I would use the encyclopedia only when absolutely necessary to write a paper, and then I would complain about it. I usually asked for Bob's help because frankly, I was not very good at finding things in the book.

Bob, on the other hand, would spend hours every day reading the encyclopedia and consuming every tiny bit of knowledge. I know that his father was pushing him hard in this endeavor, but Bob loved doing it. I ask the reader to try to think of one other person in your life who has read the *Encyclopedia Britannica* cover to cover. No wonder he was the valedictorian. That being said, I think I had more fun. Besides the competition for Colene's friendship while we were in kindergarten, there was one particular young lady that Bob and I sparred over during the entire time we were in high school. The interesting thing about the competition for this one pretty girl's favors is that, in the end, neither of us ever really went out with her in a steady fashion. At the time, there was a very good reason that we kept our distance.

When you are in your twenties or thirties, or later in life, three years' difference in age does not mean much. However, in high school, dating a girl who is three years younger can sometimes cause a stir. Suzy was one of the prettiest girls in the entire school, perhaps the prettiest, but she was young. Additionally, there were many other young men who wanted to be her best friend.

Suzy was the daughter of a dairy farmer, so she divided her time between the dairy farm, just south of town, and her home, which was in the southwest part of town. I think she preferred being a townie, but she could look great in a pair of work jeans with a T-shirt top and a bandana around her head. She certainly didn't look younger than the girls in my class. Even though I was older, when I talked to Suzie, I felt very inadequate—almost speechless. And that was not like me. She was very pretty.

Bob and I had an advantage over other guys in our amorous adventure because in addition to seeing Suzy every day in the halls of the school, we got to see her multiple times at our church throughout the week. This gave the two of us many opportunities to discuss which one of us would ask her out.

I had the upper hand in the summertime because of my job as a life guard at the swimming pool. When Suzy would climb the tower of the high diving board, dressed in a swimming suit that had shimmy shimmies on it, I had a special seat for viewing. It's good to be a life guard.

Bob and I both dated Suzy a few times, but the age difference was an issue when it came to peer pressure from the girls in our class. The boys in our class did not care, and frankly, I think they envied us. I think Suzy liked both Bob and me; however, based on some of the notes she passed to me periodically in the school hallway, I am pretty sure she liked me better. I loved to needle Bob about those notes, especially when he had just gotten an "A" on some test. I had concluded that getting a good note from Suzie was better than getting a smiley face on an essay. When graduation came and went, so did Suzy. However, she holds a very fond memory space in my young man's mind. I think I'll go find her notes in an old trunk that I have.

As I look back on the years, all the way through high school, it seems to me that Bob and I were always together. I liked being with him because I respected him, and even though I would never have told him, I envied him for his intelligence. He would also never admit it, but I think that at times he wished he were a little more like me. I was more apt to try new things, to push the envelope on legality and take my chances with the outcome. But Bob's father was the county judge, and Bob was very aware that he better not cause any waves in the community. He was concerned not only for his own well-being but for his father's reputation. It would have been unimaginable, and the small-town rumor mill would have gone wild, if Bob had ever been forced to stand in front of his father's court. However, Bob was such a straight arrow that this was never really an issue. If it had happened, it would be fun to write about.

On the other hand, hanging out with me could have been dangerous. Not that I would ever seriously break the law, but I did operate at the legal outer limits at times. I might have done things that would have caused the fine town citizens to talk.

Bob's dad, the judge, and even his mother show up many times in my childhood memories. Because of his stature in the community, I always thought of Judge Sam as one of the elite city fathers. I had also conjured up the idea that Sam must make a lot of money, so I couldn't rationalize why Bob and his family lived in a house that was as humble as my own. He called his house the "acreage" because it was on a piece of property on the outskirts of the city. Even though they had chickens and other animals, I doubt the property was even one acre in size. They did have a cow, and Bob's job was to be the milkmaid twice a day. That duty sometimes held up our playtime.

Later in life I would learn that county judges are not paid enough money for the service that they render. However, I guess it could have been worse because Sam became a judge in the post-depression days when it was more financially rewarding to get a paycheck from the county than it was to make a living as a barrister in a small town. County judges were an elected position, so Bob would accompany Sam as he traveled around Jefferson County every election cycle. Even though everybody knew Sam, and would never vote for anyone else, Sam thought it was important to look the people in the eyes. In any case, his campaigning must have been effective because he had been the county judge since the late 1930s, and he was involved in every city activity.

Sam was especially prominent when it came to youth activities, and that is where he played a huge role in my life.

He attended all the high school football and basketball games, he was a leader in the church youth organization, and he was a Boy Scout leader, just to name a few of his endeavors. Of course, Bob and his older brother were the primary reason for Sam's interaction, but I also gained from his presence. Because of his position in the community, and his political connections, Judge Sam was very helpful when it came time for me to get a college education. He wrote some wonderful letters of recommendation that highlighted what a great and deserving kid I was. He perjured himself so many times that if he had been under oath, he would have gone to his own jail.

Bob's mother was a very quiet and obviously intelligent lady who seemed to always be in the background. However, I had a sense that she may well have been the glue that held the family so tightly together as a good Christian home. Bob's mom and dad never missed an athletic event that one of their kids were involved in, even if it meant a road trip, in an old car. Periodically, they would invite me to travel with them, and that is when Bob's mom, Virginia, introduced me to a cuisine delight that I have never forgotten—the peanut-butter-and-pickle sandwich. The other family members in the car must have also liked those sandwiches because she always made them. However, Bob hated them, so I looked forward to him slipping his sandwich into my lunch bag when his mom was not looking. To this day I still love peanut-butter-and-pickle sandwiches, and any kind of pickle will do, but bread-and-butter pickles are the best.

Somewhere along the line Bob concluded that I was luckier than the average person. Perhaps that was because he could not understand how I was making it through life with such little effort while he was working his tail off. I'm not even sure why I was making it—maybe I was just lucky! On one occasion Bob decided to capitalize on my luck.

During a high school track meet, he had tied for first place in the high jump, and the officials were going to decide who got the first-place ribbon with a coin toss. I was on the other side of the field warming up for my event when Bob arrived to drag me back to the officials, so I could call the toss. Bob got the first-place ribbon—blind luck?—who knows. But Bob was happy, and my reputation for being lucky grew.

Before the day that each of us had our own cars, it was sometimes a challenge to find a friend who had their father's keys, and the gas to go with them. I did a lot of hunting in those days, and I had several friends who also enjoyed a day of shooting rabbits and squirrels, but Bob was not one of them. To my knowledge, Bob has never hunted in his life. Maybe never even shot a weapon. It might have had something to do with his dad and the law. We didn't question the idea that Bob was the only kid in the group who didn't hunt; it was just the way it was. Our preferred method of hunting rabbits in those days was to drive very slowly down a country road until we spotted a cottontail hiding in the fencerow.

At that juncture, one of us would roll down the car window, extend our .22-caliber rifle or .410 shotgun out the window, and assassinate the creature. This was a very effective and easy means of hunting, especially in the wintertime with snow on the ground. The rabbits were quite visible against the background. Shooting from a car was illegal, but that never stopped us from using a method that we knew worked. This may be why Bob didn't hunt.

One Sunday morning after church two of my hunting friends and I decided that the new snowfall was a perfect time for some road hunting. The problem was that none of us had a vehicle at our fingertips. After a caucus, it was decided that Bob would be a good fit as driver for our big afternoon. After all, he had his dad's car and he didn't like to hunt, so he could just drive and wouldn't need a turn at pulling the trigger. A perfect solution. I recall that it took a little arm-twisting to get Bob to agree because I think he sensed that there may be some illegality involved, but he finally said yes. After we had been hunting for about an hour, and we had several furry kills, we experienced an unplanned episode.

Suddenly there was a loud explosion in the car. With the windows rolled up, the noise was particularly loud, and all four of us froze in place. None of the guns were supposed to be loaded until we were ready to shoot, but that rule was sometimes broken. Besides, there had never been a problem. It seemed like forever before anyone spoke, and then everyone spoke at once, trying to find out if anyone was hurt. We were scared.

After we ascertained that no one had been wounded, it was time to determine which weapon went off, where the bullet went, and, of course, the damage. Remember, we were in the county judge's car! Looking up, there was a very, very small dark spot in the soft headliner of the Ford Fairlane, where my .22-caliber bullet had passed through. You could barely see this minor damage, so there was great relief, and we all started to laugh. The laughing stopped when we got out of the car and saw the metal of the roof peeled back. The exit wound was significant. Bob was in shock as he contemplated how to tell his dad—the judge. I was in shock because I was already known by the judge to be a bad influence on Bob. I'm not sure how the discussion with the judge went, but Bob never went hunting with us again, and from that day forward, the judge always looked at me as if I were armed and dangerous.

In a small town you usually walk or ride a bike everywhere because everything is close; in our case, they were our only modes of transportation. Bob and I lived in the same direction from the school, so after school we usually walked together for part of the way. To get from the school to our homes we had to pass through a small, hilly city park that was great for sledding in the winter and for playing capture-the-flag games on warm summer nights. On one particularly snowy school day, we were passing through the park on the way home when we spotted some younger kids sledding down a street that had been blocked off for this very evolution.

We watched the kids for a while, and then I decided that it would be fun if we joined in. Obviously we didn't have a sled, so I asked one of the youngsters if we could take a turn with his sled. I look back now and wonder if he said yes because he wanted us to join in or if he said yes because we were older and he was afraid we would beat him up if he didn't give in. I guess the reason really doesn't matter because it turned out badly.

Bob and I manned the small sled together and barreled down the hill with me in the driver's seat and Bob hanging on. We were making great speed, but instead of making the planned turn in the road, we jumped the curb and headed directly for a pond at the bottom of the hill. It was cold that day, but it had only begun to freeze, so the pond had a very thin layer of ice on it. As we approached the pond, it was clear that it was time to get off that sled. We both bailed into a snowdrift as the sled continued onto the ice, to the center of the pond, where it promptly sank. We laid there in the snow laughing until I heard the young owner of the sled screaming that we had stolen his sled. We watched him run for home to tell his mom. The next thing I knew, there was an angry mother approaching with malice on her mind. I'm not sure if I was brave or just too scared to run, but I just stood there. Bob was also scared (remember the judge), but he was not too afraid to run, and he did.

The last time I saw him during this event, he was watching my personal holocaust develop from the safety of the bushes. When the mother was done verbally abusing me, I was directed to get the sled. The pond was only two- to three-feet deep, but the water was cold, and the thin layer of ice did some serious damage on my legs as I waded out to the sunken vessel. That was the last time that Bob and I went sledding together, and I'm not sure the judge ever found out about the adventure. I was just hoping that the little kid's mother didn't know my mom and dad.

I have so many memories of those younger days, and I still consider Bob my oldest continuous friend. We were in the same church groups, the same Boy Scout troop, and on the same athletic teams. However, we were kind of an odd couple, with me just figuring out how to use the system to get by and Bob spending his evenings reading the *Encyclopedia Britannica*. I was clearly getting more from the friendship than he was, so it didn't bother me when he would shake his head in wonder after I would do something that he would never consider. He didn't even like the most wonderful snack that his mother prepared, a peanut-butter-and-pickle sandwich.

Everyone should have a lifetime friend. Try to choose one who has a "judge" for a father. It will help you survive some youthful indiscretions.

*Judge Sam instructing Bob in wilderness survival.*

## CHAPTER 5

## Freedom and Independence

———————

Watching the news outlets and daily periodicals today brings sadness to my eyes when I think about how the world has changed since I was a kid. Parents today are terrified about letting their children walk the streets alone, and rightly so. Kids are cautioned when playing on playground equipment for fear that they will get hurt. Every day there is a lawsuit against a teacher who was trying to control rowdy children. Families are warned not to eat foods that have been part of the Greatest Generation's diet for years, with no negative effects. And the list goes on and on and on. Freedoms have been lost because of fear. I wonder at times if today's children really have a childhood that prepares them for adulthood. It is just too bad that today's offspring do not have the freedoms that were present during the good-old days.

Kids in the 1940s, 1950s, and 1960s were allowed to run free and experience the world around them. I knew my parents were there to support me if I needed them, but I was trained not to need them. During the school year, you got yourself ready for school and you got yourself to school, rain, shine, or blizzard. I cannot remember a day when school was canceled—there may have been one, but I don't remember it. From the time that I was old enough to play outside, the only rule that I had was that I needed to be home before it got dark. My parents didn't know exactly where I was or what I was doing during the day, but they knew I was in town, and I'd be home when the sun went down—that was the rule. That rule existed until I entered junior high, and then it was loosened up—just a little.

The number of stories that I could tell about the independence that I had in my youth would go on forever. However, I will not bore the reader with an endless supply, only provide a few examples to illustrate the point.

By the time that I was eight I was riding my bike across town, and then across the river, for a total of five miles into the countryside to go swimming at a park called Crystal Springs. On the way back I would at times stop and fish in the Little Blue River. Nobody ever checked on me.

At about that same time in life I could walk out my back door, proceed for about a half mile on foot, and hunt with a .22-caliber rifle. Nobody ever got shot.

Starting in the fourth grade, we organized our own grade school tackle football team. The other three grade schools in town did the same, and we played each other. We set up the schedules, provided our own uniforms (a little bit of everything), and got ourselves to the games. We even officiated the games among ourselves. If there was a disagreement during the game, we worked it out. *All of this was done with no adult supervision—none.* We just made it work. No one ever got seriously hurt, and there were never any lawsuits.

During those young years, I had some wonderful compatriots who helped me search out the hidden wonders of the world. One of those people was a very special friend named Barry. Barry was a year behind me in school, but we lived within several blocks of each other, so over the years we became friends. Barry's father was a lawyer and later became a US congressman, and this special man had a great impact on my life. Like Bob's father, Barry's dad was hugely responsible for my being able to get a college education and to experience a wonderful career. Throughout the years both of Barry's parents were very good to me, and I will never forget it.

Barry was a lot like me in the fact that he loved an adventure. Together we tried many things, some of which could have killed us. But we lived.

On one occasion Barry decided, and I agreed, that we should try to build an Aqua-Lung. We probably saw one in the movies and decided we were smart enough to construct the contraption.

Luckily for a couple of young inventors there was a field full of old World War II surplus equipment right behind my house. So we decided to explore for needed parts. I know the reader is scratching their head, but, yes, it was an open field of old war surplus gear. In the late 1940s and early 1950s these large caches of new and used military equipment could be found all over the country, just lying around, deteriorating and rusting in the open weather. A fun place for young folks to play. I'm not sure if it was theft, but we found what we needed for our Aqua-Lung, and we took it. Two items were especially pertinent to the task. One was a pilot's oxygen mask, complete with a breathing hose. The other was a small pressure tank. I'm not sure what used to be in that tank, but the tank looked like something that we had seen in the movies, so we made the assumption that its previous content must have been oxygen. Who knows?

We took the tank to the local gas station and figured out how to use the tire pump to pressurize the vessel. Again, I have no idea how much pressure that tank should have been able to withstand, but we put in as much as the air station pump would allow. The next task was to assemble the rig, which we did mostly with tape. There was no duct tape in those days, so any tape at hand was used.

Because Barry was a much more accomplished salesman than me, I was chosen to test the apparatus. We conducted the first test in the basement of Barry's home. We found a large wash tub that could handle about eighteen inches of water, wide enough so that I could hang onto the sides and still thrust my head totally under water. The test didn't last long, but we proved that the mask didn't leak much, and the system seemed to work because I did not drown.

Now that the phase one test was complete, it was time to move on to operational testing. The logical location for the next phase of testing was at the country club swimming pool. Barry's family was a member, and I was allowed in as a visitor. This visit, in itself, was a big deal for me because I was not normally allowed on the club premises.

While some of the more sophisticated town ladies watched from poolside, I donned the rig by strapping it to my back with an old belt. Then I cautiously proceeded to the bottom of the pool. I had no idea how you were supposed to breathe through that mask, so I improvised. The mask was never designed to be used underwater, and my face was too small, so it started to leak. The other problem was that because of the tank, I was very buoyant and unable to remain on the bottom unless I hung onto the pool drain. From topside, it must have been quite a show, as I would hold the right side of my mask in place while holding onto the drain with my left, then I would quickly shift hands to accomplish the task on the other side.

I sat there as best I could on the bottom, holding the mask to my face, but I was not stopping the inflow of all the water. It seemed like a long time, but Barry's time recording indicated that it was only three-and-a-half minutes before the water level in the mask was intolerable. That was long enough to declare success, and to congratulate ourselves on being inventive. No adults were involved.

One of my favorite adventures of youthful freedom was the annual river raft trip. This was not an event involving many people, just two, just me and Barry.

As we approached the Fourth of July holiday, Barry and I knew that it was time to start gathering the needed materials for the building of our raft. Every year there were important lessons learned about raft building, and we always applied those lessons to the next year's event. Some of those lessons were simple, like a bigger raft is better. Other lessons were lifesaving and included items that young adventurers didn't originally think about, like bringing raft patching materials.

The first stop in procuring what we needed was at the local BF Goodrich tire store. The owner knew us well because of previous adventures. He always provided us with a large, used tractor-tire inner tube. The tube usually had a leak in it, but that was not an issue for two industrious teens. A little bicycle tire patching material and we were good to go. After the first year's raft trip, that patching kit became part of the ship's loadout.

The next stop was at the Planning Mill. The Planning Mill was the town lumberyard where my grandfather was employed as a cabinetmaker. Grandpa was the source of the wood planking we would need to build the raft's platform. As I write this, I'm again not sure that this lumber was procured legally or after dark. Too late to ask Grandpa, but who cares.

Barry's backyard was normally the location chosen for the raft assembly. His yard was bigger, and there was fencing to provide some cover so the other neighborhood kids could not see what we were doing. Even at that age, we understood that knowledge was power, and we were not about to give away the secrets of successful raft building

Using baling twine, we would attach the wood planks across the width of the inflated tractor-tire tube. Depending on the size of the tire, the raft platform would ride six to ten inches above the water line when we were underway. The draft of the vessel was barely one to three inches, and that was perfect because the Little Blue River could be a bit shallow in places, especially in July. The paddles were nothing more than thin boards that had been part of the Planning Mill heist. With raft construction completed, and the Fourth of July holiday fast approaching, it was one of our mom's job to get us to the launching point. The Little Blue River runs north to south in that area of Jefferson County, and as it passed through the town, its energy was captured by the local utility company to generate the town's electricity. Our adventure always ended near the town, so timing was everything. If you are being carried down the waterway, through the town, in a motor-less craft, the secret was to get off the river before you arrive at the dam where the utility company was located. Once you got off the river near town, you hiked the three-quarters of a mile to Barry's house to announce that you were successfully home—mission complete. The normal motherly response was, "OK, did you have a good time?"—nobody seemed worried.

The designated mother would watch as Barry and I secured the raft to the top of the family automobile. Nobody ever said, "Be careful, don't scratch the car," but I also don't remember scratching the car. The two of us and the raft were then delivered north, up the old river road, for a distance of about six to seven miles.

After the offload, the mom would leave, not to be seen again until we crawled out of the river, in town, five to six hours later. I hesitate to describe my hometown area as desolate, but during that five- to six-hour trip we would not see one other person. It was freedom to the max for a thirteen-year-old. We would float for a while and then fish for a while. We always took some supplies, so when it came time for lunch, we would put into a sandbar and dine. Barry and I had a lot of time to talk, mostly about girls, sports, how to better next year's raft, sports, and did

I mention girls? We had a great time, no one got hurt, no one got lost, and two boys learned a lot about being independent.

Barry and I didn't see each other much after high school, but we always stayed in touch and visited from time to time. He went off and became an important financial wizard. I continue to believe that the freedom that we enjoyed every Fourth of July was instrumental in his understanding of the business world. We learned to accomplish a lot, with very little, and that is how successful people make it in life.

Every year when the Fourth of July rolls around, I get an urge to build a raft.

The years have not been kind to this piece of paper, but it has historical significance. It is the sports page from my sixth-grade gazette, the class newspaper.

It says we had a successful football season, going undefeated. It lists the scores of each game. Below the scores are the names of the players, by position. Bob and I are listed as the right and left halfbacks. Together, we scored a lot of points. No referees; just kids having fun.

## CHAPTER 6

## Employment

––––––––––

The lack of money in our household was always an issue when I was growing up. Mom and Dad both worked very hard, and we never went hungry, but it was clear from listening to my parents talk, there were things that we were just not going to have. I learned early on that asking for things was not an accepted practice. I think that this is the reason that I started working at an early age. I wanted and I needed my own money if I was going to be able do some of the things that I wanted to do.

My mother used to tell me the story that during one of our first Christmases as a family, my dad went to the bank and took out a loan so that we could have presents. The thought of having to take out a loan for Christmas presents brings tears to my eyes, even today.

Well into my high school days a phantom Santa used to drop a treasure of toys at our front door during the holidays. Later I would learn that one of my dad's friends, who was a toy buyer for a local department store, would bag up all of his toy samples at the end of the year and leave them on our porch. It never crossed my mind that we were the recipient of a welfare type of gift. I just felt like the luckiest kid in town.

I don't remember a time in my life, since I was about eight years old, that I did not have some kind of employment. There were periods of time that I had multiple jobs at the same time. I didn't find it to be a burden and actually enjoyed the fact that I was working. Having your own income is very rewarding.

The following pages record some of my employment adventures, and more importantly, lifetime lessons learned.

**Gardening**

My first experience in making some cash was in the gardening business. I was not old enough to get steady employment, but after watching the neighborhood ladies working around their flower plots, I knew I could do it just as well. I soon found out that I was wrong. Even weeding a flower garden requires a level of knowledge that I did not have at that time in my life. After I experienced some aggressive leadership by one woman employer, I realized that if one is to keep his job, pulling weeds is an art form that needs to be practiced. If you are unable to pull the weed out by the roots, you better be ready to dig the root out. Just pulling the top off the weed was grounds for discipline, and a possible cut in pay.

Later I would graduate into the lawn mowing business, and that is where I started my upper-body-building routine. In those days, you did not have a power mower unless you were a well-heeled city father. The mechanical push mower was the tool of the day. A push mower is not too hard to handle on the flat ground, but if you find yourself on a hill, you had better be ready for some exertion. Nebraska has a reputation for being very flat, but I swear that all my clients lived on hills. In the winter these same hills were a blessing because my customers couldn't get in and out of their garages until they hired me to scoop snow from their driveways. The businessman in me used to inflate the prices after very heavy snowstorms. Probably something ethically or politically wrong with that, but I needed the money.

## Neighborhood Business

My brother was the second child in the family and was six years the younger, so we didn't see much of each other during my older school years. However, when we were both young, Randy was a valuable asset in building my bank account. Randy was afflicted with a bad case of asthma when he was very young; fortunately, he grew out of it completely by the time he was eight or nine years old. My mom got very disturbed when she found out that I had been making a little cash, charging the other neighborhood kids five cents each, to watch Randy run around the front yard until he started to turn blue. Mom's disgust was one thing, but I decided to immediately give up the endeavor after my dad started to retrieve his belt from his pant loops.

There were many kids living within four or five blocks of our house, so there were other ample opportunities for a businessman. After some thought, it came to me that weekly boxing matches might be in order. With a stubby pencil and some paper, I listed all the boys by their approximate size so that I could pair them up in the ring. I am still amazed that I could talk these kids into beating each other up every week and paying me, the promoter, to do it.

Early on, one fight-scheduling issue did arise. However, with a little bit of ingenuity I was able to solve the problem. Dale, who was only one year younger than me, was extremely small for his age. Even smaller than me, so he was really small, but he was wiry and fast. I had to go to the edge of the envelope to find him a competitor or I was going to lose one of my matches, and a little cash. Even though he was five years older than my brother, they were a good height and weight match, so that was the decision. I loved my brother very much, and I would have defended him until the end against anyone in a street fight, but this was business. Every Wednesday, until the kids got tired of paying me, Randy would climb into the makeshift ring and Dale would beat him up.

I'm sorry, Mom—really, I'm sorry.

## Paper Routes

When I was ten, I applied for and was hired as a paperboy for the local newspaper. The Fairbury *Daily News* was a six-day-a-week periodical and was read by citizens throughout the county. It wasn't a very big paper—only six or seven pages—but it had all the information that you needed for your day-to-day decisions: everything from the weather report to the price of wheat and how much hogs were selling for. Every once in a while one of the town troublemakers would get drunk and start a fight or have a wreck, and that would be headline news.

The newspaper owners had divided the various areas of town up into routes, and there must have been ten or twelve of us boys who did the deliveries. Because there were only a finite number of routes, I had to wait until one of the older boys moved on to another job before I could be hired. I'm not sure how I won the next opening because the competition was fierce.

Every afternoon around four thirty the carriers would assemble at the back double doors of the news office to await our individual supply of papers. Even today I can shut my eyes and enjoy the aroma of the printer's ink as the presses were spinning out their product. Much of that ink was transferred to my hands by the time that the day's delivery was complete

Each day before I arrived at the back door to get my papers, I had a ritual where I would stop by Hested's Five and Dime store to fulfill my candy fix requirement. My preference was a half-bag of candy corn and half-bag of salted peanuts. I would mix these two ingredients together so that each handful was sweet and salty. Additionally, I would purchase a Coca-Cola in one of their now-famous bottles. I wasn't allowed to buy a Pepsi because my dad sold Coca-Cola. Somehow he would have found out. After several sips of the Coke, I would pour the candy and peanut mix into the bottle, causing a heavy fizz. There was something very special about the subsequent swallows of Coke as the liquid flowed around and over the salt and sweetness. Chewing the mix also seemed to be very satisfying.

Spending that fifteen or twenty cents a day on candy probably was not a good business decision, but it was a decision that I could afford to make.

Along with the other carriers, I would sit outside the big double doors of the *Daily News* and fold the papers, then load them into the newspaper bag that was wrapped around my bicycle handlebars, all the while swigging my Coke, peanut, and candy corn mix.

I diligently folded my papers and enjoyed my first classes in sex education as I listened to the older guys discuss their various sexual adventures. It seems that there was one particular young lady in the Park School district who the guys knew quite well. I never did meet her, but I sure did gain great knowledge about her during those discussions. Sometimes it pays to just listen.

A couple of years later, I would supplement my income by taking on an additional paper route with the Lincoln *Star*. The *Star* was to be delivered in the morning, so it required an early wakeup call. It fact, I would climb out of bed at four thirty every morning and pedal my bike to the Rock Island Railroad train depot. As I have discussed, Fairbury is not a big town, but I lived on the north side and the depot was on the south side. I made this two-mile trip every morning, regardless of the weather, and I can attest to the fact that there were some significant snowstorms during my youth. Fortunately, it was all downhill because I remember those mornings as cold, dark, and lonely.

The only other person at the depot at that time of day was the sleepy station master. He wasn't a very talkative fellow, but he at least said "Mornin'." I would wait on the platform or walkway next to the tracks for the arrival of the Rock Island *Rocket* at 4:52. In those days Fairbury was one of the main stops for the *Rocket* on its trip from Omaha to Denver, and my supply of journals was on that train. The *Rocket* never stopped for very long, and I don't recall many people ever getting on or off. The door from the baggage car would open and a strong arm would throw out a bundle of papers and the train would leave—my day had begun.

After gathering up the bundle, I would return to the depot where I'd sit and absorb the heat of the potbelly stove while I conducted my paper-folding process. After the train left, it was extremely quiet, and my guess is that the station master went back to sleep. Just me and the quiet was OK.

My first delivery was at the far western end of town, so the second leg of my daily pedal was another mile and a half before I reached my first house. I remember some seriously big and unrestrained dogs in that part of town, so arrival in the dark of night was always a challenge. I am convinced that these dogs would purposely wait in hiding until I was about on them, and then they would spring. One large black mongrel was of particular concern, so when I approached his neighborhood, I was on high alert.

One morning, as I cruised slowly onto this particular canine's street, my head was on a swivel, but the creature had outwitted me by hiding behind a different bush. As I got right alongside the shrub, he growled, barked, and launched himself at the bike. I was terrified because this dog had gotten me once before, and I have the four-inch scar to prove it (by the way, there was no lawsuit). When he launched, my adrenaline kicked in, and I started pedaling as hard and as fast as I could, and then there was a loud scream of a wolf-like nature. Rover's tail had gotten caught in the sprocket of the bike, and as I kicked the bike into high gear, the tail was amputated. The black giant never bothered me again, but from time to time I'd see his stubby butt hightailing it out of my way. The owners of the dog were clients of mine, but they never mentioned the episode. I think that PETA and the lawyers would be heavily involved today.

By the time that I was close to completing my rounds, it would be getting light. So, in the summer, I'd take a little time to collect night crawlers for afternoon fishing. Especially if had rained the night before, these large worms would have emerged from the ground and would be abundant in the street gutters. I always kept a small coffee can in my paper bag just in case. All you had to do was scoop up the wiggling creatures. Dad was always happy to see me arrive home with a can full of bait.

The last stop on my route was at my maternal grandparents' house. They only lived a few hundred yards down the alley from my house, so stopping for breakfast just seemed logical. Besides, it would save Mom the effort of cooking for me. Grandma was always waiting to feed me breakfast, and it was always the same because I wanted it that way. Two pieces of toast with homemade strawberry jam and a glass of freshly squeezed orange juice was a great start to each morning.

My dad's parents lived in a house that was so small that it is hard to describe, so trust me when I say small. The house was heated with coal and had only one grating where the heat entered the house. My place to dine was right over that grate, sitting in an old chair with my plate on a foldout metal TV table. It was a very warm way to finish off my daily business, before getting ready for school.

## Golf Caddie

Because we were not members of the local country club, I had no idea who played golf or if anyone was any good. In fact, I had never been on a golf course or held a ball or club in my hand. That's why it was interesting when I was contacted about carrying a bag during an event, involving what I referred to as "cow pasture pool." The town grapevine announcing who was a hardworking kid must have been active because the gentleman who called me was the husband of one of my previous weed-pulling clients.

It seems that Byron, who lived just up the street, was actually a very good golfer and had won many statewide championships. I did not really know

Byron, but I had seen him over the years and I was floored when I heard about his golf prowess. I knew he was a successful executive at one of the town's bigger businesses, but he didn't look like a person who could successfully swing a golf club. At that time he was probably in his mid- to late thirties and short in stature at about five and a half feet tall, but he weighed over 350 pounds. I've heard estimates of four hundred pounds. However, I was about to find out just how graceful this big man could be when hitting a little white ball. I was astounded by the beauty and grace of his golf swing, and when he put all his weight into the shot, that ball would go a long, long way.

During practice sessions, he would send me out to a specified distance to stand in one place while he would hit balls at me. He instructed me that after he hit a certain number of balls, I was to collect them and return them to him so he could hit to the next distance. There were no practice ranges at some of the places that he played, so I became his personal range. He made my ball-recovery job very easy, though, because I didn't have to move much. I would just stand in one place and catch most of the balls as they were hit. I would simply hold out the ball bag— he would hit the balls, and the bag would fill up. He was very good.

Byron did not need any help from me during a round of golf except to carry the bag, and that was good because I didn't know anything.

There were two types of golf tournaments played during my caddie days. The first was on grass greens as we know them today, but the greens were not nearly as nice. The second type was on what were known as "sand greens." Most people today have never heard of sand greens, but they were prevalent in small towns that did not have enough money to install and maintain grass. Sand greens could be messy because it was normally a very fine sand with an oil solution base. Before you putted, you needed to drag the path that you were going to putt on so it would be smooth. When play on the green was complete, my job was to rake the entire green. When I was done, it looked just like a flat sand trap looks today.

I had clearly hitched my cart to a winner. Byron won every match he played that summer, and finished it off by winning the state grass and sand green tourneys. Later in life when I took up golf and found out just how difficult a game it is, I developed even more respect for Byron. When I think about that big, nonathletic-looking man destroying the competition, I want to go out and practice.

He was like a Minnesota Fats taking an unknowing customer apart and relieving him of his cash. Never judge a book by its cover is great advice.

## Car Parts

I was lucky enough to land a job as a stock boy at an automotive sales company early in my high school days. I had just bought my first car, and it needed a lot of attention. The seventy-five dollars that I spent on the 1949 Chevy was not out of my reach, but over the next few years I replaced almost every moving part in that car. The Chevy had originally been owned by the Union Pacific Railroad, and it had been driven hard over many country roads. Actually, at times I think they must have driven it on the tracks and the railroad ties themselves. The first problem for a young dating teenager was the color of the vehicle. It was a very faded reddish hue, and on the front doors you could still see the outline of the Union Pacific logo. Even my dad agreed that this could not stand.

My dad worked for the Coca-Cola bottling company, and he was able to convince his boss to let us use the back half of the warehouse for our car painting effort. Dad came up with a paint gun, and we turned that Chevy into a black beauty. We had to find a color that would cover the logo, and also, I think black paint was the cheapest.

Over the next two years, Dad and I would spend a lot of time under the hood of that car. We replaced the engine once and the transmission twice. The clutch was a continual problem and required replacement three times. All of the parts necessary for these repairs were procured at the local car salvage yard, at minimal cost. Mr. Paneitz, the owner of the salvage yard, didn't charge much if you were willing to scavenge the field to find a similar wreck and then remove the parts on your own. Dad and I knew where every wrecked 1949 Chevy was in that salvage yard, and we became experts at stripping them of usable parts.

After two years, I declared that it was time to move up in the auto chain, and Dad agreed because he was worn out from fixing the Chevy. The automobile sales company that I was working for had a 1951 Ford on the used-car lot, and it was perfect for my next vehicle. It was not exactly what I was looking for, but the $150 price tag made it close to perfect.

I was looking for a car with a V-8 engine, and this particular model was just a flathead six. I was hoping that the girls would not notice the total lack of power displayed by my new muscle car.

My dad rested because the Ford did not require as much attention. I drove the Ford for over five years and only gave it up when I left the state to attend college. I think my brother drove it for a while, but its final destination is unknown to me. I will say that many good times were experienced in that Ford. You could go a long way on a gallon of gas in a six-cylinder, and with periodic gas wars at times I was paying only twelve cents a gallon.

My duties at the car dealership did not require much brain power. When one of the mechanics would say "Go get me a part," I went and got it. Fairly simple. However, I did garner a lot of knowledge about cars, and I see that period in my life as one that added greatly to my worldly education.

Even though he looked much older, one of the mechanics was a fellow who was only about three or four years older than me, but he could fix anything. I had not known him well before, except I knew he had left high school to go to work. I'm embarrassed to say now that in the beginning he was not the kind of person that I would normally associate with. But after a few months, we became friends. I guess he liked the way that I went and got him parts. He would tease me about my duties of running for his parts and sweeping up the shop and his mess. At the same time he would not hesitate to teach me about cars. By the time that I moved on from that job, there was not much about Fords that I could not fix.

Another example of a book's cover being deceptive.

## Driving Hogs

The livestock sales barn is a very important part of any Midwestern town's economy, and it became another link in my personal employment chain. The sales barn usually operated two or three times a week, and it was where livestock were bought and sold. One day would be for cattle sales and another would be for hogs. Once in a while there would be a day for horse sales, but that was unusual in Fairbury. The sales barn complex covered a large amount of acreage and was made up of a sales pavilion and multiple covered buildings that contained holding pens for the animals. Farmers would arrive early in the morning and off-load the animals into an assigned pen, awaiting their time to enter the sales ring.

When I was very young, my maternal grandfather would take me to the barn on sales day to witness how he bought and sold his animals. I remember that the hotdogs they served in the lunch area were the best that I had ever tasted. I know it offends some, but the smell of all the animals and the stench of manure was very soothing to me. It was like a back-home aroma, and one that made me feel safe and comfortable. If I concentrate, I can still smell it now.

I was very taken by the sight of the young calves as they entered the ring and the bartering began. After a few trips to the barn with Grandpa, and a lot of badgering by me, he agreed to buy me a calf just because I thought it was cute. Over a period of time I watched that calf grow up as if it were my own, and then one day in the fall, it was time to butcher. Nobody asked my permission, and I didn't say a word, but that was the last farm animal that I ever bought.

Because of my youthful experience of visits to the barn on sales day, I understood how the barn operated. However, when I first went to work there in my fourteenth year, I was initially hired by a construction company to assist in putting a new roof on the sales barn. I ran nails and lumber for the real craftsmen who were doing the work. Seems like most of the jobs that I was hired to do during my early years started off as a "gofer."

During one of my first days on the job, I had a near-death experience. I was carrying a ten-foot-long piece of lumber across a roof that was being repaired. I'm not sure why, but at the time I was walking backward across the slanted roof surface with the board sticking out five feet on either side of my body. Suddenly, the bottom dropped away from me as I inadvertently stepped into a skylight opening. The abrupt stop that followed this fall saved me from continuing twenty feet to the ground below. I'm sure that there would have been some serious bodily damage if I had completed that fall. The five feet of lumber on either side of my body was enough to catch on the sides of the opening, and my grip on that board was superhuman. There I hung, and a lesson was learned. Watch where you are going if you don't want to step into a hole!

Being around the rough-and-tumble laborers on this construction site was an education. I assembled a new lexicon and learned to yell at everyone. The crew chief was a huge man named Spider, and everyone knew that he was the boss. However, he was always pretty nice to me. On one occasion he told me to go get the one-ton truck from the other side of the barn and bring it around to the front because it was full of lumber that they needed. There were two problems with this order. First of all, this was a big truck with a big clutch and a lot of gears, and I doubted that I could sit in the seat and touch the pedals. There was a second problem that I tried to explain to Spider, but he wasn't listening. I had just turned fourteen and had never driven anything in my life. He bellowed, "Go get the damn truck!"

I know that I was gone for a long time, but I finally got the truck started. There was a lot of gas pedal pumping and choke pulling before the engine finally turned over, but I had seen others do this very thing, and it worked. The next challenge was to get it into a forward gear. I would slide down, off the seat, so I could push the clutch in, and then move the floor stick shift. I was lucky on the first try to get it into a forward gear because when I pushed my body back up onto the seat and peered through the steering wheel, the truck had already begun to lurch forward. I was probably in the lowest gear possible because the transmission was making an enormous noise.

I knew there was not going to be any additional shifting going on because I didn't want to slide down under the steering wheel again to push on the clutch. With me at the controls, that truck arrived on the other side of the barn in the same gear that it had started in. As I approached the work area I slid off the seat and pushed on the brake. The engine died, and I leapt out of the truck like that is how I had planned it. A great cheer went up among the workers and Spider was pleased, with me and himself, as I saw him snicker. After that day, I was considered one of the boys. Today I realize that everyone needs a Spider in their life.

After the barn roof was completed, I was able to extend my employment by getting hired by the sales barn leadership. My new job was to herd animals during sales days. When there are a lot of huge animals to be moved from place to place, you need folks to make sure those animals get to the correct destination at the right time, and that was going to be my job. The orchestration and timing of moving the animals from their pen to the sales ring was one to be marveled at. I had watched this evolution many times with Grandpa, and I knew I'd be good at it.

The assistant to the auctioneer would give me three animal pen numbers, and my instructions would be to deliver whatever was in those pens to the sales ring, in the proper sequence. Other "drivers" would be doing the same thing with their three numbers, so you needed to work around everyone else's movements. When you completed your three deliveries, you went back and received three more, until everything had been sold. You did not want to get caught with your animals on the same driving path as another driver, especially going in opposite directions.

A short explanation of what "driving" really entailed is probably in order because there was some danger involved. All of the animal pens opened up into a long fenced path that was referred to as the "chute." The chute led from the animal pens to the sales ring that was housed in the sales pavilion. As the animals entered the ring, the auctioneer would announce something about the age and source of the creatures and those would be the last words out of his mouth that I understood. I could only marvel as he would break out into a lingo that only a seasoned buyer and seller would understand. I would know when the sale was complete when I heard something like "Sold to number twelve for three hundred dollars." That was my cue to get those fuzzy beasts out of the ring so the next ones could enter.

The danger in this job normally came while you were driving the animals in the chute. You needed to keep all the animals headed in the right direction, and it was usually on the run. If they ever got spooked or decided to turn around, you could be in big trouble. If the animals ever reversed course on you, it would resemble the running of the bulls as you attempted to leap over the fence in an attempt to get out of the way. Not only could you get hurt, but you could really screw up the sales sequence because of the delay.

You haven't lived until you've experienced a three-hundred to four-hundred-pound hog coming at you at high speed in an enclosed area. It is even more exciting when you only weigh 110 pounds. If you can't get over the fence, you need to be prepared to take a blow that could not be duplicated on a football field. The hog's head goes down like a running back as he plants his nostrils in your belly. From then on, you are just along for the ride. If you slip off his head, you will get trampled by the whole herd. It hurts my professional ego to admit that I have experienced this embarrassment on several occasions. My high school English teacher was right when he used to say, "Never wrestle with a pig. You will just get dirty, and the pig loves it."

**Farm Jobs**

Every boy that grew up in the Midwest has worked on a farm, at least from time to time. My grandparents were Kansas farmers, so I had experienced the rural lifestyle from a very young age. The closest town to the farm was inhabited by a population of fifty, and when you went to town, you went on a tractor because the roads were usually otherwise impassable. More discussion of growing up around the farm has been addressed in another chapter, but suffice it to say here, any and all work completed on a farm is damn tough and will make a young body strong.

Unlike today, where much of the farm land is owned by large conglomerates, in the mid- to late 1900s most farms around my hometown were owned by family farmers. Some of these were as small as a quarter of a section, and that was only 160 acres. On that relatively small piece of Mother Earth the farmer would attempt to provide for his family. Besides being hard work, there were always challenges, and some could be of biblical proportion.

There could be too much rain so that the crops rot in the field and you can't get in the field to harvest. There could be a drought and nothing will grow or the output of the harvest is diminished. A hail storm could be devastating, destroying the plants at any stage of their growth. Bugs and disease are always a threat. In those days, the means to control them was not readily available.

Most farmers around Fairbury were dryland farmers because there was limited access to irrigation. The area around Jefferson County had wonderful soil for growing crops, but fate had dealt the county a mighty blow. Jefferson County was situated just outside the dimensions of the giant underground Ogallala Aquifer. The aquifer stretches from the Dakotas to Texas and is enormous in size, but its watery gold stops just short of Fairbury. If you went twenty miles to the northwest of town, you could put down a very productive well. Good wells around Fairbury were very hard to find. Mother Nature usually determined if farm families survived the year.

It is against this backdrop that young boys like myself would seek work under the employment of the local farmers. Even though the farmers were stretched for cash, they needed help because if they didn't get the crops out of the field at the correct time, it was a losing situation.

The backbreaking job of hauling bales of hay from the field to a barn or to designated stacking areas was one of the primary requirements for hired labor. A day of hauling bales of hay was great work for those of us who were preparing for an upcoming football season. Depending on what kind of hay had been baled, and whether it had been baled when it was wet or dry, the bales could weigh anywhere between 65 and 120 pounds each. The hayrack, or trailer, was usually pulled by a tractor, but I can remember using horses or mules. The hayrack would be slowly pulled though the field while we would walk beside it and throw the bales up to be stacked to maximize the load. There was usually a bale on the ground every ten to fifteen feet, so you were constantly in motion. The bed of the hayrack was normally about three feet off the ground, and each bale was fifteen to eighteen inches high. As a result, tossing the first layer of bales up was not a big challenge. However, as the hayrack filled up and you got to the point where you were throwing heavy bales up three or four levels, you were waiting for someone to say, "That's high enough. Let's go unload."

There were always other chores that the farmers needed help with, and I can remember many a day that I spent putting in fence posts and stringing barbed-wire fence. I would usually get directions on what needed to be done, and then I wouldn't see the boss (farm owner) until the end of the day when he would come by to inspect. Digging holes on a hot Nebraska summer day, with no one to talk to, will give you lots of time to reflect on what you want to do with your future. It was clear to me that even though I had great respect for them, I did not want to be a farmer.

From time to time you could get the cushy task of riding a tractor, usually to plow or harrow a field after harvest. Riding a tractor in the hot summer sun beats every other farm job that you can imagine. There is no physical stress, except it makes your back hurt from all the pounding as the tractor travels over the rough ground.

The act of plowing turns the soil over to aerate it and to plow under the stubble, or residue, from the harvested crop. This helps to return nutrients to the earth in preparation for next year's planting. Harrowing, or discing, is breaking up the dirt clods that you normally get while plowing. Again, this was an effort to loosen up the soil and make it more workable. Harrowing was like what you would do in a garden to break up the soil with a rake.

I vividly recall my last farm job and that last two weeks I spent in a dirty Cornhusker farm field because it was a part of the story that changed my life forever.

During the previous year, I had been lucky enough to get an appointment to the United States Naval Academy in Annapolis, Maryland. For a kid who had never seen a pool of water bigger than a hog trough, going to the Naval Academy was going to be a welcome, but serious, change. It was also a hallelujah episode for me and my family because it was a free education. As the day approached for me to depart for school, I realized that even though I would eventually get reimbursed for the trip, I did not have the $32.50 required for the airline ticket from Omaha to Baltimore. The word spread throughout the congregation of the First Christian Church that I needed a short-time job and I needed it now. Mr. Fox, like the good Christian that he was, stepped forward, and for two weeks I did his every bidding. I never saw him again after leaving Fairbury, but wherever you are, thank you, Mr. Fox.

**Printer's Assistant**

The last few years of my high school were filled with as much employment as I could get. I knew that if I were ever going to attend college, it was going to be on my own personal ticket. There were times that I was working two jobs at once, and the most money that I ever made during that time was seventy-five cents an hour. As a young dating teenager, my bank account did not fill up very rapidly.

Earlier I described the Hested Five and Dime store chain that was headquartered in Fairbury. Mr. Hested, who I met early on while mowing his yard and scooping snow from his driveway, had founded the chain of stores and was probably the richest guy in town. At one time there were over 115 Hested stores throughout the Midwest. I always found it interesting that this little town could be the source of such a successful business, but entrepreneurs can come from anywhere. At least they could in those days. Because of the vast array of items that were sold in a five-and-dime, advertising was a must. All the pamphlets and brochures, etc., for this advertising were printed on two small printing presses located in the back room of the headquarters building.

I don't recall how I landed the job, but I became the assistant to the man who ran those printing presses. Louie was an easy boss to work for. He was a diminutive man who always had a smile on his face, a smile that suggested he thought he knew something no one else knew. His laugh was one of those that was very distinctive, high-pitched and a little bit evil. There may have been things going on with Louie that I was not smart enough to figure out at that time in my life. But he was fun to work for, and I was getting my seventy-five cents an hour.

For a one-week period of time during my printer's assistant tenure, I found myself in charge of the entire printing operation. Being propelled into a leadership position occurred because of an eye-opening episode.

From day one on the job, Louie had cautioned me to be very careful around the running presses. We never wore loose clothing that could get caught in the moving machinery, and there were only a few places that you wanted to put your hands when the press was in motion.

Normally, I was always facing away from Louie's work area, as I remained focused on my printing press and the product that I was turning out. The fateful day that I became the printing press boss for a week was no different. Little did I know that the day was about to get exciting. Suddenly, I heard Louie yelling. Now yelling and other loud noises out of Louie were not unusual because he was always singing, laughing, or yelling to be heard over the noise in the room. But this was a different kind of yelling. When I looked over my shoulder, I saw him standing there holding his hand and screaming. In the beginning, I didn't pay any attention—this was just Louie being Louie.

When I turned back again, I was stunned to note that Louie was missing a finger. Later, with his wry laugh, he would love to tell folks that it was his middle finger. I sprang into action and put a tourniquet around what was left of the digit. His hand was a bloody mess, and like all printers, his hands were black with printer's ink. After we got him off to the hospital, it was my job to clean up the work room and, of course, continue the printing jobs.

As I was cleaning up at the end of the day, I was surprised at how little blood was on Louie's press. But my guess is that it was so mixed up with ink that I just couldn't see it. All of a sudden, I stepped back from the press and stared because there was Louie's finger lying under one of the trays. After putting the finger in a bag, I remember calling the executive who was in charge of the building to report my find. I have no idea what became of "Louie's fifth," but when he returned to work a week later he was laughing. He was a weird but happy little man.

## The Muny Pool

It is always good to have a job where one of your primary duties is to watch pretty girls. As long as the pretty girls are part of the population that you are trying to save from drowning, it is perfectly fine to watch them, and that is the job of a lifeguard. For five wonderful years I had this job at the city municipal pool, which we fondly referred to as the "muny pool."

Throughout the time that I worked at the pool, my boss, the pool manager, was also my high school track coach. He had also been my junior high football and basketball coach. Being a jack of all trades, Harold was also the assistant principal of the high school. The bottom line is that I knew him well. He was such an important part of my teenage years that he is deserving of, and will later have, a chapter of his own.

For the purposes of this section, let's just say he was a great boss, mentor, and friend. He always made sure I got extra hours of work because seventy-five cents didn't add up very fast. One of those extra jobs was the cleaning of the pool area before the daily opening.

It was during these morning cleaning sessions that I got an education on the cleanliness habits of the two sexes. The men's locker room was as you might expect. Candy wrappers, chewing gum, and abandoned jock straps were present, as well as many unflushed urinals and toilets.

The women's locker room was a different issue, and I hated cleaning that place. I was stunned by what was left lying around on the floors and benches. I doubt that these feminine items would have been left adrift at the girls' own homes. If they were, I think that both mom and dad would be grossed out. I used a lot of chlorine bleach in the women's dressing room.

The pool would remain open until nine p.m. daily, but there was always work to do after the doors were locked. For example, the water filtration system needed attention as we headed into the overnight hours. That duty was also assigned to me, which gave me another chunk of hours to log on my worksheet. When the pool closed, we would put the water filtration system on back flush for about three hours, and then it would need to be returned to the normal filtration mode just before midnight. This gave me enough time to go on a date, see a movie, have a hamburger, and then return to the pool for valve realignment

Besides getting a few extra working hours doing the valve lineup, there was one other benefit to having this duty. Young ladies were always impressed that I could offer them an opportunity to take a midnight swim in the muny pool. We all knew it was illegal, and if the coach had found out, I would have been a dead duck. Fortunately, nobody ever discovered us. There were times when the city's finest police officers would pull up to inspect the premises while two young, scared souls would cling to the pool side until they were gone. There was always a great deal of laughter after their departure, and in the eyes of the young lady, I was quite a rebel.

As typical teenage lifeguards, I doubt that we took our jobs seriously enough. As a result, Harold would periodically remind us that just because no one drowned yesterday doesn't mean that no one will drown today or tomorrow. Although we never had a drowning, this was good advice because from time to time we needed to pull a swimmer out. Pulling a frightened swimmer from the water always got our attention and caused us to focus for at least a few days.

Because the sun was so hot, we would change guards every hour and a half. When not actively sitting guard duty, we took turns selling "gedunk," checking people into the pool, or cleaning up around the perimeter of the pool. Gedunk was our name for candy and soda pop, which was fondly referred to as "Cokey pop" or "Pepsi pop."

Being sent out to conduct perimeter cleanup could be fraught with danger. Every once in a while we would identify a "floater" in the shallow end of the pool, where the little kids would hang out. The floater might resemble a Baby Ruth candy bar, but it was not. We had a special net that was used to rid the premises of floaters, and at the end of the day the floater net received a large dose of chlorine cleaner. Fortunately, we had a lot of this cleaner on hand.

Being identified as a lifeguard also offered an opportunity to supplement my income when I was hired to teach swimming lessons. The little kids were easy to teach because you could instruct them all together in a class environment. They seemed to learn at the same pace, and by the end of the sessions the mothers were pleased. However, there was another category of nonswimmer that was a lot more interesting to teach. They didn't learn very fast, but they were a lot more fun to teach.

From time to time I would get a request for lessons from an adult who did not know how to swim and was embarrassed to enroll in the larger class format. All of the requests that I got came from women, some young mothers, others from girls who were only one or two years older than me. I also recall that at least two of these girls had been on my radar screen for a long time as beauties, but they were older and clearly way out of my league. These lessons were always privately held and went much more slowly, but the students always learned to swim.

Seems strange, but just giving those lessons helped me move up the social ladder.

## Employment Summary

By the time that I graduated from high school, I had been working for ten years. I had bought my own cars, paid for my own insurance policies, paid for the clothes that I wore. I had funded all the activities that I took part in and saved a little money to start college. But most of all I had learned much about the human race and how to deal with people. Every kid should have this kind of start in life

I learned that "If you meet a man who knows how to do a job, you will have met a man who will always have a job—but if you meet a man who knows why the other man is doing that job, you will have met his boss."

I wanted to grow up to be a boss.

*Organizing a neighborhood football team and then charging participants to play—genius. I'm the one standing in the middle.*

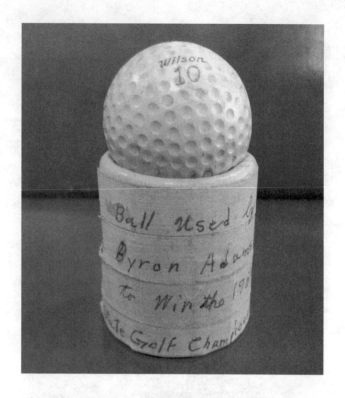

This is the golf ball used by Byron to win the 1954 Nebraska State Golf Championship. It has traveled many long miles in my "sea trunk."

*I spent many seriously cold early Nebraska mornings at the Rock Island Depot, waiting for the train to deliver papers from Lincoln. My day would begin in the dark.*

*The Rock Island Depot is now a wonderful museum. The benches that I used to sit on and fold papers, before my paper route began, are a reminder of the long and useless discussions I had with the station master. I would talk, and he would grunt.*

*Great memories of delicious hamburgers, the smell of the farm, and the chant of the auctioneer as animals were bought and sold.*

## CHAPTER 7

## Youthful Impressions

———————

There are always those times in your life when you hear about something or you witness something that makes a huge impression on you. These happenings may be momentary and fleeting and seem to only be a footnote when compared to the entire history of your life. However, even fleeting events have a way of causing you to reflect on what and why something just happened and, more importantly, cause you to think about if there is a lesson to be learned.

Even though I tried to hide it, I was a very impressionable young man. So, as my youthful days passed, at times I found myself wishing that I could be more like some people and at the same time being thankful that I was not like some others. The same was true as I watched classmates do things that I considered cool, wishing that I would have had the idea or the guts to do it myself. Of course, there were the classmates who did some really dumb stuff, and all I could think about was that they were in real trouble. I learned some of my most important lessons of life when I or classmates did dumb stuff.

## Alvin

Except for the fact that I was terrified of catching polio, there was not a whole lot that physically scared me when I was growing up. Those were the days of no cure for polio, and the dreaded "iron lung." Just the thought of forever being imprisoned in that machine caused me to shudder.

My life, in and out of school, revolved around physical activity. Most of it was exercise and games that today are considered too dangerous for the youth of America. As an example, in the dark of the night we would play capture-the-flag in one of the city parks. The game pitted two teams in an exercise of trying to capture one another's home base, while not getting caught by the opponent. The game was best played when there was no moon and, of course, no adults around. I can remember many times impaling myself on a water sprinkler as I sprinted from hiding place to hiding place. This was a war without weapons, and it was important to win, so you picked yourself up and continued the operation. At the end of the night, when we mustered to count heads to make sure we were all alive and well, there were various bruises, sprained ankles, and cuts from thorns, but we were all present.

Even in grade school, physical activity was the centerpiece of our day, and I don't recall the teachers restricting how violently we played the games. A quickly organized game of kickball at playtime could result in some serious collisions, and that is where I first realized that the human body was not invulnerable.

Alvin was not the biggest kid in the class, but he was the most well built for strength and endurance, even at the age of ten. He was also the fastest person in the school, and therefore the first choice when teams were being established for any game. If Alvin was on your team, you were probably going to win. Until one warm spring day in the sixth grade, as far as I was concerned, Alvin was indestructible.

That all changed for me one day during a school recess period. As Alvin sprinted down the sideline of the schoolyard on his way to another goal, his progress was suddenly interrupted by Jimmie. Jimmie was not as fast as Alvin, but he was bigger, and when they both occupied the same space at high speed, there was a mighty collision. Alvin went airborne and exited the playground, passing over the top of a bush hedgerow and down a steep incline. After a momentary hush from all of the participants, we peered over the bushes to find our athletic superhero with what would turn out to be a broken collar bone.

Seems like such a minor event in the big scheme of life, but I have never forgotten that day and the damage that was done. Alvin went on to a very successful high school and college athletic career. I was left with a much clearer lesson and understanding that I wasn't as tough as I thought I was.

If Alvin could get hurt, so could I.

## Ms. Mudge

In a small town you usually end up going through all twelve years of your schooling with the same kids, and you get to know them very well. Early on, it becomes clear who is the smartest, who is the strongest, who is the fastest, and in some cases, who to steer clear of. That being said, even though I had known her since kindergarten, I had no idea that

Judy was one of those people to avoid when she was angry. I doubt that our sixth-grade teacher, Ms. Mudge, knew it either. She and the whole class were about to get a lesson in "loss of classroom control."

As compared to the many excellent teachers that I would have while growing up, Ms. Mudge had to be rated at the lowest end of the scale. Sixth-graders are not the best people to be rating their elders, but it was clear from the beginning that we were going to be a difficult mission for this struggling teacher. She had been teaching for years, but her abilities were questionable. Kids can be very mean, and my guess is that we were typical, but my sixth-grade year was the first and last time that I ever saw us show hostility toward adult supervision.

My recollection is that Ms. Mudge only had two dresses. It didn't make any difference to me and the other boys, but the girls in the class found this to be a significant source of ridicule. One day she would wear a dark green one, and the next day it would be a wine-colored one. The following day, the cycle would repeat itself. If she had at least been an average teacher, my guess is that no one would have found her dressing habit to be unusual. Heck, I only had one pair of jeans and a single white T-shirt that I wore every day. Judy, the major player in this short recollection, was a big girl and towered over all the other kids in the class. She was not only tall. If there had been a weight-lifting contest, there would have been no contest at all. Judy was very strong.

All that being said, Judy was a very shy, quiet, and friendly person who got along with everyone. She was an average student, but she struggled with some subjects. And that was the rub. Ms. Mudge had apparently decided that Judy was either not smart, or worse, was not trying because Ms. Mudge had taken to harassing Judy during class time. The obviously condescending harassment had gone on for months and had been the subject matter of many schoolyard discussions. However, the discussions always ended with a shrug and an agreement that we kids could do nothing about it. History will reflect that we were wrong.

The day of the great sixth-grade revolt started like any other day, with Ms. Mudge trying to teach and the class not listening very well. When the day progressed to the time when Judy's harassment would normally start, the only difference noted was that Judy began to cry. That did not seem to faze the irate teacher as she came closer to Judy's desk, with her voice reaching to almost screaming levels and her face shaded in crimson.

Then the world turned upside down. In shock, the class watched as the gentle giant of a sixth-grader rose up from her desk and found herself towering over a now terrified teacher. It was nose to forehead, and you could tell that today was going to be different. It was so quiet as Ms. Mudge stared up into Judy's eyes. Nothing was said, but Judy began to shake, and in an instant, it was over.

There was a crashing right hook to the jaw, and Mudge went to the floor. Then it was really quiet. I remember thinking how much trouble we were all in. I was pretty sure that just being in the class was going to ensure that I was guilty of something, and I probably was. The next school day, Judy was back in class as if nothing had happened.

I'm sure that the previous night was filled with parent-teacher meetings, and perhaps a school board meeting. But there we were, back in class, as normal.

Ms. Mudge finished that school year with my class, but she never again demeaned anyone. We all just went through the educational motions for the rest of the term and were glad to be through with each other at the end of the year. My class went off to junior high school, and Ms. Mudge started with the next year's class. She never finished that school year and was removed from teaching by higher authority. Probably best for everyone.

On that fateful day, I know it would have been better if Judy and Ms. Mudge had both just walked away. On the other hand, if they had, would the problem have been solved? Would the harassment of Judy have continued? Would a bad teacher still be teaching?

The fact that this single event still occupies a space in my memory indicates that I must have learned something that day.

## The Ram Rods

Organized gangs of law breakers and troublemakers were not something that was prevalent, especially in small Midwestern towns, during the 1950s. The fact that everyone knew everyone else, and usually knew what everyone else was up to, was not a good environment for gang-like activities. It was difficult to go out and cause trouble when the whole town knew who did it. The town had a small police force, but if the officers knew exactly which door to knock on, you didn't need many officers to uphold the law.

That is one of the reasons that it was so unusual when the Ram Rods suddenly appeared as an organized motorcycle gang. In the beginning, the organization appeared to be composed of the usual suspects: every young person in town who owned a motorcycle. The members would meet on a street corner or some other designated location and then ride as a group around town, sometimes holding up traffic but not really causing any trouble. To my knowledge, the gang never directly threatened or intimidated any other of the town's citizens. When discussions would break out about this "so-called gang," the members would simply emphasize that they were a motorcycle club and nothing more.

The leadership of the Ram Rods was an unknown for quite a while, but it was assumed that the head of the group was a rather imposing high school class-mate who was an excellent football player but not so accomplished in the classroom. However, after a while, the rumor started to spread that perhaps the jock was just the muscle and the real leadership lay in the hands of another classmate. Not that it was a surprise that Barbara was part of the gang, but it was surprising that she had taken over the reins of leadership. However, in retrospect, it shouldn't have been because Barbara, now known as Sadie, was smarter and more street savvy than the rest of the gang put together.

I had known Barbara as a friend since our kinder-garten days, and she had never been a troublemaker. However, in her later teens, she had taken a different route in life from most of her classmates. Sounds like a silly, simple issue now, but she started smoking at a young age and started hanging out with a suspect and shady bunch of characters. At least, they were clearly different from most of her classmates, and that is how she inherited the new moniker of Sadie. She didn't own a motorcycle, but she was obviously directing traffic from the back seat of one.

As time passed, there were more and more unconfirmed stories of the Ram Rods conducting hostile takeovers of bars within short riding distances of town. There were numerous small towns of only fifty to one hundred citizens within fifteen to twenty miles, and they were easy prey for an organized gang of thugs.

Stories of the gang entering one end of these small towns and running the citizens out of the other end of town were being discussed on the street. The stories sounded a little far-fetched to me because I had never seen the gang do anything bad. But the gang's reputation started to spread. At the time, there was a recording that was being played by the radio disc jockeys depicting wild birds and animal sounds emanating from an obvious jungle scene. One of the Omaha announcers used to introduce the playing of the record by saying, "These are the sounds of Fairbury on Saturday night." The town leaders decided that this was not a good reputation for our town, so the crackdown commenced.

I have no firsthand knowledge of exactly what went down, but gang members started to disappear from the streets, and the gang's activities started to diminish. Soon, it was over, and the Ram Rod's former existence was no longer discussed. My belief is that there might have been some jail time for certain characters, but I don't know who or how much. Shortly thereafter, Sadie left town.

I remember thinking that some of the activities that the gang were supposedly involved in were cool, and I thought that I'd like to be part of it. Then I'd hear the adults discuss what was going to happen when the gang was finally brought under control. I was pretty sure that staying on the straight-and-narrow road was the best path for me and that I was not cut out to be a bandito.

**The Rumble**

Fights between small Midwestern town teenagers were not a usual occurrence in the 1950s. Word of an altercation would travel so fast that by the time you got home, your parents and everyone else in town had more knowledge of the event than the fighters themselves. Knowing the personalities and the previous parental corrective actions, this was not a good thing to come home to.

Because of this parental deterrence, I have to admit to being surprised at what happened one night during my junior year. Social media in those days was simply word of mouth, and normally the student jungle drums were fast. Therefore, my biggest surprise was the fact I did not know that the fight was going to take place until it was in progress. I should be embarrassed because, as it turns out, everyone else in the school knew about it.

The two major characters in this one-act play were named Johnny and Gary, but they were not going to be in combat against each other. They were on the same side. Even though they were not in the same school class, with Gary being a couple of years older, they had been the very best of friends for years. Both were excellent athletes, and they had been outstanding leaders in their respective classes. Additionally, both young men were extremely handsome and always had the best-looking ducktail haircuts in town. They dated two of the prettiest girls in the school, two sisters, one of which was a classmate. All in all, Gary and Johnny were two of the older guys whom I tried to emulate socially and athletically. I admit to envy because of how cool they were.

It is important to understand how we got to this evening of the grand finale, because our two warriors had been planning this event for over a year.

Friday nights are high school sports nights, and rivalries between some towns can be intense. The rivalry on the court or field will usually decide a winner, but sometimes losers want to continue the battle after the final whistle. This whole episode started a year before the rumble, during an away game. Johnny and Gary had been spectators at the game and had been confronted by three of the opponent town's overly aggressive rooters. It seems that the aggressive rooters attempted to draw my two heroes into a fight. In most cases it would not have taken much to stimulate Gary and Johnny to defend their hometown's honor, but that night, one year before, was different.

Unknown to the aggressors, Johnny and Gary were both in training as members of the town's Golden Gloves boxing team. Both were very accomplished in the fine art of defense, and it was expected that the team they led would eventually do very well in the state competition. If Johnny and Gary had chosen to fight, I'm confident they would have prevailed. However, on that night, they chose instead to let the thugs cast aspersions on their manhood and push them around.

The reader may ask, why would they not defend themselves when it was clear that they had the capability? I don't want my dad to know this, but I can tell you from painful experience that a bareknuckle fight can be very destructive to many parts of the body, but mostly you can easily break your knuckles and fingers. Even the worst fighters have an extremely hard face.

Johnny and Gary knew that if they fought, the possibility existed that they could damage their hands. They would have risked their Golden Glove dreams and the town's chances of winning. And so, they took the abuse. But they also did not forget. That started a yearlong planning session to avenge themselves. Now, here we were at the day of reckoning, the night of the rumble.

Young folks don't always make good decisions, so I have always marveled that these two gladiators, in the heat of battle, made a proper decision that benefited not only themselves but other team members as well.

One year later the scene took place after a basketball game and sock hop, a dance that the school had organized for the students. Mostly, the sock hop was to keep us off the streets after the game. Students who had traveled from the visiting town for the game had also been invited, so there was a cross section of both team's supporters at the dance. But there was no trouble, and everyone got along in congenial and friendly fashion. There was no indication that a conflict was on the horizon. I didn't even know that the three lads who had embarrassed Johnny and Gary the year before were in the crowd.

However, Johnny and Gary knew, and they were waiting outside in the street for the party to be over. By the time I exited the school, the thirty-yard-long sidewalk leading from the school front door to the street was lined on both sides with students, three or four bodies deep. When the three previous year's perpetrators stepped out of the school door, it was the first time they sensed danger. They had put last year's fun behind them and didn't realize that their fate had been in a 365-day planning cycle.

At the school end of the sidewalk stood three terrified young males. At the other end, standing in the street, were Johnny and Gary, looking like ominous characters out of the movie *Blackboard Jungle*. Both were dressed in blue jeans, heavy black boots, white T-shirts, and black leather jackets. Their ducktailed haircuts were properly greased up, and they looked mean, but cool.

It was so quiet that when Gary finally spoke, he didn't have to yell to be heard all the way to the school front door. His words were a simple explanation of why not last year but now this year. He then issued an invitation for the three to join him and Johnny in the street to finish the matter. It got even quieter as all eyes were on the lads, but they seemed frozen in place with fear.

I don't think most folks in the crowd understood what had happened the year before until Gary delivered his message. So when the three didn't move, the gathered students began to yell and taunt. Mob rule was suddenly in effect, and the boys knew it, so they slowly started down the path to the street. Gary and Johnny met them with angry words and a lot of pushing, but no punches were thrown. It was obvious that the three were too scared to fight because they recognized the outcome. It was their turn to be humiliated with rhetoric and shoving. Gary and Johnny seemed to also sense that they had won without a fight, and they were enjoying the frightened bodies in front of them. But it was not over.

The three edged their way through the crowd, and it turned out to be a huge mistake. As the visitors scrambled inside and started their car, suddenly baseball bats appeared. The escapees were unable to avoid damage to every car window before their vehicle roared down the street and out of town.

As the crowd dispersed, excitingly discussing what had just happened and what the repercussions might be, another vehicle was noted parked at the end of the street. A city police car, containing two of the town's three officers, had witnessed the entire event. By morning everybody in town knew what happened, but there were no repercussions, and small-town life went on.

The town's police force was also the sponsor of the town's Golden Gloves team, and they must have known what was going to happen for the whole year. The decision had been made at an official level to just let this thing work its way out. I guess it's good to know folks at city hall.

I can't condone the outcome, and "rumble" is probably a mischaracterization of the event. However, Johnny and Gary continued to be two of my heroes as they provided yet another building block in my life's experiences.

As a postscript, Johnny and Gary did not win the state Golden Glove Championship that year, but they did make the finals, and that was a huge accomplishment for our little town. They had made a very serious and adult decision in delaying the altercation, and it worked out well. Both Johnny and Gary became very successful in life. One became a dentist and the other a college professor. A small-town success story.

## The Death

Death is something that you don't spend a lot of time thinking about when you are young, at least I didn't. People were always dying, but not the young. They were old folks, and most of the time I didn't really know them. The only way that you knew that someone had died was when you heard your parents talking about it or you saw cars slowing down in front of Nuckolls Mortuary to read the obituary posted in the glass announcement board by the street. Except for my deep fear of catching polio and then spending the rest of my life in an iron lung, I didn't worry much about life's end.

That changed in a significant way on an early Sunday evening during my sophomore year in high school.

The story starts with Dennis—not me, another Dennis. Dennis was a high school classmate, but not the kind of kid that I knew very well or that I would hang out with. I had known him since the fourth or fifth grade but only by his reputation and a few personal "run-ins." I went to Central Ward for my elementary school years, and Dennis attended the Park School, where the kids were known to be a little on the tough side. We Central Warders always knew that when we played Park in football, win or lose, it was going to be a rough game. Those games were played without a referee or adult supervision, so rule infractions were common, with a lot of arguments about who did what to whom.

Maybe because I was small for my age, or maybe because we normally won the game, Dennis had decided that he didn't like me very much and that I needed to be beaten up. His need to thump me resulted in several occasions when he would corner me after the game, after my teammates had departed. That gave him the opportunity to push me around some. He never did really hit me, but I know he was hoping that I would swing so he had the excuse he was looking for. I knew that if I took a shot at him, I was going to lose the fight, and then I'd have to face my dad with the results. Neither of those outcomes was very interesting, so I let Dennis shove and push me around.

Church activities during my high school years were something that I really looked forward to. I'm sure I was picking up some religious knowledge, just because of my constant exposure to biblical stories. But truthfully, I enjoyed going to church functions because all my friends were there. Besides Sunday school and the regular church service on Sunday morning, there was a Sunday evening youth group that I attended. Another excuse to get out of the house to be with friends was the Wednesday night youth fellowship meeting, and I was always there.

I'm not sure why, but on this particular summer Sunday evening I arrived at the church earlier than normal, when there was still no one else around. As I rested on the church front steps, I could hear an ambulance siren in the distance, and that ominous sound always gets small-town folks interested to find out what's going on. I am no different, so as I stood up, my initial thought was that I would get in the car and go search out the action. After all, just being sixteen with a brand-new driver's license was excuse enough to drive anywhere, at any time.

By the time that I reached my car it was obvious that the siren was getting louder, so I waited and watched as the ambulance came into view and stopped right across the street from the church. The Lynch Clinic, where I was born, was the ambulance's final destination, and the hospital staff must have been waiting because the building doors flew open.

Personal reactions during catastrophes, accidents, problems, episodes, or just strange events are interesting. I normally would have stayed in front of the church and just watched from a distance. However, before I knew it, I was standing right next to the ambulance as the big back door of the vehicle swung open and they started to roll out the gurney. The face of the person on the mobile bed had been badly damaged, and the white sheet that partially covered the body was red with wet blood, but I could tell that the still body was that of Dennis.

The ambulance personnel were working very fast to get the gurney up on its wheels and the victim secured in place before rolling toward the clinic door. Dennis's arms were just hanging over the side of the gurney, so one of the attendants pulled the arms up and crossed them on his chest, and the movement toward the hospital began.

The gurney had moved only about twenty feet when the sight that has been with me for many years occurred. Both of Dennis's arms just loosely dropped from his chest and fell over the side of the gurney, dragging on the ground as the gurney moved. Nobody would have to tell me about this event in the morning. I knew then that Dennis was dead.

Dennis did not like me, and I did not like him, so I'm not really sure why this episode has stayed with me so long.

Perhaps it is because there was a great lesson in automobile safety coming out of this horrible event. Dennis's car had left the road at high speed, and a tree branch came through the front window, spearing him. Maybe I had just seen death, up close and personal, for the first time, and I realized that it didn't make any difference that we hadn't liked each other.

*The sidewalk leading from the front door of the high school to the street was lined with students the night of the rumble. Johnny and Gary stood in the street, prepared for battle. The visiting students were terror-stricken as they exited the door and walked to the street.*

*An interesting side note—the school has now been converted into an apartment complex. Someone is living in my old math classroom.*

## CHAPTER 8

## Family Pets

——————

Having pets around the house seemed like such a normal thing that it never crossed my mind that some families did not. I loved the family animals and so did my folks, but I think my parents put in a lot more animal maintenance time than I did. There was always the requirement to walk the dog or pick up some kind of a mess that had been created. And, of course, there was the never-ending and huge piles of fur in every corner of every room. I don't think I was a very good zookeeper because Mom was the one who seemed to always get the detail.

Dogs were the animal of choice in our house. There never was a cat in the house until my sisters came along because Dad didn't seem to take to felines very well. However, later in his life he began to mellow, and you would catch him watching TV with a cat on his lap. But he didn't want that story told around town.

Dad did like birds, until we got one. In fact, I think Dad was the one who brought Petey the parakeet home from the Five and Dime store. For the first few days the family marveled as Petey flew around the house, landing on people's heads and enjoying his new home. The fun was short-lived when Dad found out that Petey was using various places around the house to relieve himself. After that revelation, Petey was restricted to his cage, and the family enthusiasm for his presence wore off. Petey died of old age in that cage and was not replaced with another feathered friend.

As the animal of choice, there was always a dog in our house. And when one would pass due to old age, he was quickly replaced. We didn't know much about pedigree animals, so all of our dogs started their life in a litter born in the barn of some farmer. The word would quickly get around town that someone had too many puppies and that new homes were needed, and quick. At the time the word "quick" didn't mean much to me, but later it would. When you went to get the puppy, you usually had to slosh through a muddy farmyard and then climb into a corncrib or barn to find the new hounds. There were no "best in show" animals here, but they made great pets.

Curly was the first dog that I can remember being part of the family. He was part this and part that, but mostly he looked like a cocker spaniel. From the day Curly came home, he kind of had a chip on his shoulder. The look in his eye seemed to say, "I'm going out and kick some ass." That attitude was a problem when Curly would get out of the house.

We lived on the edge of the town, and there were acreages, or small farms, not too far from our front door. Not sure where it was developed, but Curly had acquired a taste for chicken, and he preferred to kill it himself. Therefore, as soon as Curly could get through the front door, he headed straight for the neighbor's henhouse. We paid for a lot of dead chickens, and they were too chewed up for us to eat. Curly was never broken of his appetite for poultry, but he found himself under house arrest for the rest of his long life.

Dad had always wanted a Labrador retriever. He talked about it all the time. When Curly passed, I was sure that a Lab was going to be my next best friend, but that didn't happen. When Dad found out that

Labs cost money, we headed back to the farm for a free replacement

The next dog in a long line of canines was Toby, or as my friend Bob used to call him, "Tobias hound." Toby was kind of a wiener dog, but he had a strange-looking body and face. His body was long, but not as long as it should have been. His legs were short, but not as short as they should have been. His body was covered in short, shiny brown fur, except for his face. He had very long and unruly hair on his snout and chin. He looked like he had a perpetual five o'clock shadow and he needed a shave. Dad and I would trim him up from time to time.

Toby did not look much like a Lab, but he had a wonderfully long life, and he never chased a chicken. Dad was happy.

Suzie was a beagle and actually even looked like a beagle. She had all the proper markings, her body size was correct, and she could howl with the best of them. I think, from day one, Mom liked Suzie better than all the other animals that had crossed the threshold. Suzie was easy to like. She was a lovable dog, and the first female animal that we had owned. Mom liked that.

It was this motherly love that almost did Suzie in. Mom had decided that Suzie looked a little thin and that she needed extra meal rations. Suzie started getting meals between meals. Over the weeks, Mom watched but did not see the weight gain that she expected. Suzie remained at the normal beagle size, but still too thin for Mom. After consultation with Grandpa and Grandma on the farm, a new plan for Suzie's diet was concocted. One that is not recommended by the better chefs.

Calf supplement is a mixture of high-protein ingredients that farmers feed to cows, horses, and pigs to increase their growth and weight prior to sale. It basically increases the calories per mouthful, and trust me, it is very effective. It is even fed to goats, rabbits, and poultry, but it was never intended for dogs. Mom did not read the fine print.

Suzie went on a calf supplement diet, and then Mom saw results. It wasn't long before Suzie looked like a huge cylinder, with tiny, skinny legs sticking out the bottom. In proportion to her body, her legs looked like toothpicks. Within days, we had to take the dog-feeding duty away from Mom, but the damage was done.

Try as we might, and we even tried starving her, we could never get Suzie back to her svelte body form. That being said, Suzie lived a long and loving life. Mom always felt bad about Suzie's "condition," so they spent a lot of time together, talking. Mom always liked Suzie better than most of the other animals.

I had to be careful about having pets or being too friendly with animals on the farm. Being on the farm could be harsh, and you might find yourself eating one of your playmates. Grandpa said it was just the way of life.

There were always dogs and cats around the farmyard, but I don't recall that any of them were allowed in the house. The cats, especially, were feral in nature, and they would tear up your arms and face if you tried to be too friendly.

Grandpa would not comment on the number of dogs and cats that inhabited the place until the number got so big that it could not be ignored. I'm not sure how Grandpa determined the number that was "too many," but he knew what the number was, and that was good enough for him. After all, farmers don't have a real fondness for animals that don't work or produce money. If you are an animal that is just eating and taking up space, you are in the head count when Grandpa said "Too many." If Grandpa started oiling up his rifle or started to look for a gunnysack full of rocks, you knew something bad was going to happen. Grandma would try to give away as many animals as she could, but every other farm had the same overhabitation problem. In the end, something bad would happen, but Grandpa always tried to shield me from it.

Of course, I knew what had happened, and from time to time, I would cry. Very slowly and precisely, Grandpa would look me in the eye and explain why it was necessary to periodically cull the herd. I was too young to do anything but cry. However, I came away from those discussions understanding that Grandpa didn't want to do what he did, but to him it was necessary.

He was right when he said, "Boy, there are going to be some tough decisions to be made in your life. Get ready to make them."

*Curly—the great chicken killer.*

## CHAPTER 9

## Aunt Dell

———————

Cops and robbers, cowboys and Indians, and pirates of the high seas were just some of the childhood games that I loved to play. Much of what we reenacted on Saturday afternoons was a result of what we had seen at the movie matinee. However, I also believe that my playtime was a form of revisiting history. I had always liked history, of every kind, and whenever I could hear a historical fact or story from an original source, it was like gold for my young mind. Gold in the form of knowledge is what my Aunt Dell brought to my childhood.

Della Adams was my grandfather's older sister, and having been born in 1877, was already sixty-three years old when I was born. Still, by the time that she passed away at age 101, she had made a huge impact on the content of my youthful mind. How could I not be impressed when listening to a story told by a person who had grown up in the same time period as the likes of the notorious bank and train robbers Butch Cassidy and the Sundance Kid?

Aunt Dell was born in Iowa but traveled to south-eastern Nebraska in a covered wagon when she was young. My mind would run wild when she would describe her first Nebraska home as a simple dug-out in the side of a hill. Her room, where I would sit and listen to her stories, was full of artifacts that had made that dangerous covered wagon trip with her family. She kept her belongings in a chest of drawers that had a very defined gouge in the front of one of the drawers. The gouge had been caused by the plow that had been packed next to the chest during the journey. As the covered wagon traveled over the rough prairie, the plow slowly rubbed a memory into one of the few pieces of furniture that the family owned.

As a youth, she had collected Indian arrow- and spearheads, along with tomahawk parts, from actual Indian camping grounds. These artifacts of history were proudly displayed on a counter in her room for us kids to view and wonder about. As I grew older, I calculated a plan that would allow me to eventually take custody of these wonderful items before my siblings and cousins beat me to the treasure.

A battered and dented kerosene lantern that had been part of her family's household effects during the journey still sat by her bed until the day she died. As the sun would set, the glow from this antique lamp cast a smoky and greasy halo around the rocking chair where Aunt Dell would sit. I knew at the time that the presence of that hot and flaming old lamp was a fire hazard, but no one ever voiced a concern or tried to alter its use.

Ashby Adams was Aunt Dell's husband, and he died when I was young. But I do have fond recollections of one of his prized possessions. He must have been one of the movers and shakers of the 1940s because he owned this really neat Ford coupe with a rumble seat.

Saturday night was the big shopping time in Fairbury because the stores remained open until nine o'clock and all the farmers would come to town to get their weekly supplies. My folks and my grandparents also did most of their shopping on Saturday evenings. In almost ritualistic fashion they would arrive downtown early, so they could each park their cars in the same parking place every week. I never understood why that was important, but it was. Uncle Ashby parked on the east side of the town square, right in front of Brown's Shoe Store. Uncle Ashby and Aunt Dell would sit in the two front seats and nod and greet the shoppers as they passed. Everybody knew everybody else, but folks always seemed happy to see one another after a hard week's work. To my great joy, I was assigned to sit in the rumble seat while my parents shopped. I'm sure that I was placed there as a babysitting tool, but it didn't matter because being in that fancy car, watching my whole world go by, made me feel pretty special.

When Uncle Ashby died, Aunt Dell moved in with my grandparents. My grandparents' house was not just small, it was very small, so alterations were necessary so that Aunt Dell could have her own room.

The original house size was maybe nine hundred square feet, with one bedroom. However, its small size did not deter twelve to fifteen of us from crowding into that house every Sunday for a family dinner. The addition of another bedroom on the back of the house was an easy fix because grandpa was a carpenter and he could build anything. When he was done, the house had grown by another one hundred and forty-four square feet. Aunt Dell lived in that tiny addition and carried on all the activities of her life for the next thirty years. It was in this room that I learned so much about the way things had been and why our family was the way it was.

In those days very few people in town, or on the farm, had much disposable income. Everything that was purchased was done on a day-to-day and week-to-week basis, and that included food. It was particularly true of our family, so there was an effort to set up stockpiles of food whenever the assets became available. It seemed like we were always canning a vegetable or fruit or slaughtering a steer or hog in preparation for the winter. Our family was like an ant hill of activity all summer during the growing season.

Clothing was another item that was rarely purchased new, and more than likely I was wearing hand-me-downs from my older cousin. Aunt Dell came to the rescue when a new clothing item was truly needed. Through the years she had developed an expertise as a seamstress, and she was actively employed by many families in town to make everything from dresses to trousers and even sport coats. Her little bedroom was draped with partially completed clothing articles, and you could hear the sewing machine spinning the minute you walked into the house.

When my cousin got married, there was no money for fancy clothes, so Aunt Dell made the white tuxedo jackets that were worn by the groom and those of us in the wedding party. I'm sure the jackets were not as good as store-bought, but I couldn't tell any difference, and I looked pretty special that day.

Aunt Dell was also the family barber, so we usually had to move sewing items in her room before each of us got a trim. I was well into my teens before she started to lose her sight, and so for safety reasons, we needed to find someone new to shear our locks.

Even as her eyesight failed, she remained in her room of a thousand uses and attempted to sew and read by using a large magnifying glass. The eyesight left her, but her mind remained keen, and history discussions were still important to me as I sat at the foot of her old rocking chair. I don't recall all the discussions, but I do remember the gist of every session. She never used these exact words, but it was clear to me that if I didn't understand the lessons that history could teach us, I was probably doomed to repeat some stupid event. Aunt Dell was worth listening to.

*My grandparents, Almon and Mary Jones, are on the left.
The lady on the right is my grandfather's older sister, Della
Adams (aka Aunt Dell). After my grandfather died, my
grandma and Aunt Dell lived together in the little house
behind them for over twenty-five years. Twenty-five years is
not bad for two people who didn't get along very well. They
both lived to be over 101.*

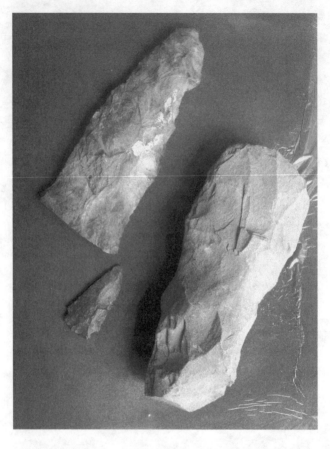

*A tomahawk, a spear point, and an arrowhead—some of Aunt Dell's wonderful Indian artifacts.*

## CHAPTER 10

## The Wreck

My junior year in high school was one of those good years. Carolyn Kay was my girlfriend, I was doing well in school, and I remained reasonably competitive in all the school sports programs. The only weak link in my existence was the constant lack of cash, which prevented me from being the big man on campus that I wanted to be. At the time my car was a 1951 Ford that was not in the best of condition. Additionally, it only had a six-cylinder engine, so it didn't make that deep-throated exhaust sound that you got from the more powerful eight-cylinder engine. For some reason girls preferred to go on dates in a more powerful sounding car. I reasoned that they equated noise to money. After all, bigger engines used more gas and, therefore, the owner must have more money. At least that is what I thought.

My dad was driving a 1953 Plymouth at that time, so it didn't help me to move up the social ladder by asking for the keys to his six-cylinder chariot. However, Dad's car was in a little better shape than mine, and it was two years newer, so I would periodically try to impress Carolyn Kay with upgraded wheels.

The Plymouth came into play one very chilly October Friday night after a football game. I had cleaned Dad's car up, and the plan was that following the game, my friend Gerald and his girlfriend Deanna would join Carolyn Kay and myself on a double date. There were no specific plans for the evening, but all four of us knew that eventually there would be a little "closeness" involved. What I didn't bargain for is what would happen during the football game. There was a very talented senior who was the starting quarterback on the team, and frankly, he was so good that if Pat didn't play, we didn't win. I was his backup at the position, but because of his prowess I was not getting much playing time. That all changed in the second quarter of the game when he went down with a severe knee injury. The rest of the game story does not take long to tell. We lost badly, and I took an enormous physical beating before that game was over. By the time I had showered and exited the locker room, I could hardly walk. Not only was I physically beaten up, I was extremely tired, and that set the stage for what would be one of the worst nights of my young life.

I felt a little better after a big hug from Carolyn Kay. Additionally, after a short four-person consultation, it was decided that no one really wanted to go to the Youth Center or sit down somewhere to eat, so we would simply take a drive in the country. The town was so small that it only took about thirty seconds to get to the city limits, and driving in the country was a usual event because the drive normally ended up in parking the car on a dirt country road for some of that closeness.

With Carolyn Kay next to me, we headed south out of town on one of the better gravel roads in the county. Gerald and I were hoping for the time that we could pull over and stop, but you need the right moment of agreement on that issue, and it just never seemed to come. The radio was blasting 1950s-era music, and everyone was talking loudly at the same time, trying to be heard over the beat of Dad's AM radio. After we had gone a few miles, it was suggested that it was getting late, so it would be best to reverse course and head back to town. I loved being with my friends, and especially Carolyn Kay, but I remember thinking how tired I was and that going home was a great idea. The evening was coming to a close, and there was no reason to hurry, so I was only driving about thirty or thirty-five miles an hour as we passed Crystal Springs, a local fishing park, about two miles from town.

It was then that I'm missing about ten to fifteen seconds of history. I must have fallen asleep because the next thing I remember is the steering wheel pulling hard to the right as the right front wheel was caught up in the heavy gravel piled along the edge of the road. I could feel the car going to the right, and I jerked the steering wheel to the left to compensate. Big mistake. The car started a slow roll, almost like slow motion, over the embankment to the right, and all I could do was hold on in horror as I realized what was happening.

The scene when the car came to rest on its right side was bizarre from my vantage point. The headlights were still on and shining mysteriously up in the air. The radio was still playing away, and the car heater was blasting hot air into the car because the engine was still running. The only human sound inside the car was Deanna, half laughing and half screaming in a hideous fashion. Vision within the car was impossible because of all the dirt in the air.

I very quickly realized that I needed to find out the condition of my friends, so I reached up and shut off the engine and the radio. I couldn't see a soul, and Deanna had now stopped making any sound, so in the quietness I asked if everyone was OK. Carolyn Kay said that she was, but she wanted out of the car—NOW. Deanna just said yes, she was OK, but Gerald announced that he thought he had a problem with his ribs. As the car had rolled to the right, the back door had come open and Gerald started to slide out. The car then rolled onto the door, abruptly slamming the door shut and into Gerald's side. Fortunately, it only resulted in a significant bruise.

The driver's side door was pointing straight up into the air, so after kicking it open, we all crawled up and out of the car. By the time we climbed up the embankment to the road, there was another car waiting there. Another classmate, Mary Lou, and her boyfriend had been right behind us on the road and described watching and wondering as our car veered to the right and disappeared over the edge of the incline. Mary Lou and her boyfriend were ready to take us back to town, but before we left the scene, I climbed back down to the car to shut off the lights.

Now that I knew that everyone was OK, I was afraid that the next worst part of the entire episode was ready to begin. I was about to face my parents, and especially my dad, to tell them that one of their few possessions was now a wreck. Dad had a history of not taking surprises well, and this time I had to agree that he would have every right to light off on me. I was sure that this was going to be a bad encounter.

Mary Lou dropped the girls off, and Gerald went with me to inform the family. I'm not sure why he went. I think his logic was that he could verify that I had been going slowly and had fallen asleep, perhaps cushioning the blow of the announcement.

I decided that this news was not going to get better with age, or with an attempt at an explanation, so I got right to the point. Mom was in the kitchen, and Dad was in his usual place watching TV as we came into the house. My first words were "I wrecked the damn thing," and then I stood by for the blast. But the blast didn't happen. Dad calmly looked up and asked, "Is everyone OK?" Mom walked in and asked, "Where did it happen?" I couldn't believe what I was hearing, but I answered their questions while I cautiously waited for fire and brimstone. After a while, both Mom and Dad quietly said that they wanted to see the car.

Gerald went home, but Mom, Dad, and I went to the Crystal Springs road in the middle of a cold October Friday night to inspect my mess. On the way to the scene, Mom asked several times if I had been drinking, and I assured her that the answer was no, I had just fallen asleep at the wheel. It was easy to see what my folks were worried about now that it was clear that no one was hurt. By dawn everybody in town would know the wreck had occurred, and there would be speculation in all neighborhoods as to why. Mom, especially, was collecting data and getting her story ready so she could take on all skeptics. Peer pressure is one thing, but small-town peer pressure is a much bigger animal.

I still was having trouble understanding how well Dad had taken the news. This was not like him, so I was on alert for any sign that he was about to erupt.

It was very dark when we arrived at the scene, so Dad took a flashlight and crawled down the embankment to inspect the damage. At first I didn't even notice that my mom was also in the ditch, crawling on her hands and knees with a flashlight, tracing the path that the car had taken as it went over the side. Her response, when asked, was that she was looking for any old whiskey or beer bottles that might be used by others to impugn my story. I could only shake my head, wondering who in town might want to spend the next morning crawling in a ditch so they could gin up a good story to tell on a street corner. Mom didn't find any bottles, but she was now prepared for anything.

I learned a lot that night. I found out how scared you can be when you think your actions may have hurt or even killed someone. I watched my college fund go into the red after finding out the cost of the wreck. It came home to me very clearly how conscious and protective my mother was of her little piece of the town's social network. But most of all, for the first time, I saw my father as a person who recognized that there was a difference between important and unimportant issues. He could tell right from the beginning that this situation called for calm, and he was.

For so many years, when I would do something wrong, even something minor in nature, it could be ugly.

I know now that he used those ugly times as a teaching moment in the only way he knew how, and he was very effective. I usually didn't make the same mistake twice, and I attribute that to the newfound trait that I had assigned to my dad: tough but fair leadership.

## CHAPTER 11

## Doctor Bill

——————

Throughout my youth, I needed a lot of medical attention. It was not the way I planned it, but every time that I attempted something athletic, some part of my body failed. The failure was usually caused by someone much bigger than me occupying the same space, at the same time. My dad was not big on excuses, so I needed a doctor who could make rapid repairs that would get me through to the next Friday night.

That is where Doctor Bill came in very handy. He had not been the one who attended to me during my early years, through chicken pox, measles, tonsil removal, and all of the other childhood maladies. However, he became the go-to medic as I entered my junior and senior high school days.

Doctor Bill was a big man, but not heavy in weight. He was stout in structure and had the appearance of once being an athlete. He had large but gentle hands, and his bedside manner was very reassuring. I would see and feel a lot of those big hands over the years as he attempted to put me back together. He would talk to me as he worked, and he once told me that every doctor should spend time in the military. I asked why, and he just shrugged and said, "It would make them a better doctor." I think Doctor Bill must have done some time in uniform.

Doctor Bill was also a very accomplished singer in our church choir, and people were always asking him to perform at festivities. But he never did sing to me while he was in the healing mode. It's probably just as well.

He did not tiptoe around when it came time to go to work. If it was bad, he would tell you so. If it was going to hurt, he would tell you. He would ask me if I was ready before he started readjusting, but it didn't make any difference because I didn't get a vote. He was going to do it no matter what I said.

Whenever I would walk, crawl, or be carried into his office, he had that partial smile on his face that said, "So, you did it again, dumb ass." I knew he wanted to tell me to stop this athletic nonsense, but he never did. He would just wave me onto the table and prepare me for the torture.

As the years passed Doctor Bill would be responsible for fixing broken arms, legs, and toes; dislocated knees; concussions; broken fingers; and cracked ribs—which are very painful. However, the repair that I dreaded the most was the straightening of a broken nose, which, unfortunately, happened on multiple occasions.

It turns out that noses heal very fast, so it's important to get to the doctor immediately. If you wait, even overnight, you run the risk of having to have the nose rebroken just to set it. At least that is what they told me, so most of my nasal repairs were done in the middle of the night. That would get the medical staff into a bad mood before they had even started. However, Doctor Bill just nodded and went about his business. I'm glad he was there.

The reason for my dread of the broken nose was the evil tool that was used during the repair. The tool looked like a giant two-pronged tuning fork, with an equally large handle. The prongs were spaced just the right distance apart so they could be inserted up both nasal passageways simultaneously. The two prongs were pretty fat, but I have proof that they would fit up both nasal passages of a normal-sized nose.

Doctor Bill would put me in a chair that resembled a dentist's chair, and then he would lean it back, all the way. He still had one foot on the ground, but his other leg would be raised such that his knee was firmly planted on my chest. He didn't have to tell me that this was going to hurt. One of his hands gripped the tuning fork, while the other large hand pushed hard against my forehead. The cold metal prongs went up my nose and the obligatory "Are you ready?" was communicated. With a knee on your chest, a large hand on your forehead, and two prongs up your nose, there is no easy way to answer that question.

With no hesitation, he would start pulling up on my nose until I was sure that it would be amputated. When he thought he had it straight, he would pull the prongs out and view his work. He was a perfectionist and he was having too much fun, so it would take him several tortuous pulls before he declared victory. I didn't cry, but there were tears in my eyes.

After each of the "nose jobs," I vowed to protect my face at all costs. I was unable to keep my vow, so I sure am glad that Doctor Bill never moved away from town. Those large hands, gentle manner, and

good "doctoring" taught me to trust the medical profession. He put me back on the road when my body
had several flat tires.

## CHAPTER 12

# Never Lose Your Bicycle

———————

Getting around a small town by foot was not a very big deal for a healthy young man. If you decided to run, you could go from one city limit to the other in about eight minutes. Older folks might take a little longer.

That being said, it was always better to have wheels. Besides, you were at a great disadvantage in picking up groceries for your mom or delivering newspapers if you didn't have a bike. Bicycles were a huge status symbol during my grade school days, and peer pressure could be a cruel motivator. I felt that pressure often.

It was not only important to have the right brand of bike—and Schwinn was the preferred model— you needed the proper amount of bicycle decoration. The decorations that I'm talking about did not come from the manufacturer. The best decorations were carefully, and with skilled hands, added to the vehicle by its proud owner. It was important that every piece of bicycle decoration either fluttered in the breeze when you pedaled fast or made lots of noise.

Tassels that could hang from the handlebar handgrips were a favorite place to start decorating a new bike. As soon as the new bike was out of the box, it was time to carefully, without destroying the rubber, remove the grips from the bars. If you were smart (and we all were), you already had searched the house and the neighborhood for the longest, brightest multiple-colored plastic material that you could find. Plastic was important because most bikes were left outside at night and the harsh Nebraska winters could quickly disintegrate any other material. Once the handcrafted tassels had been inserted through holes in the end of the grips, it was time to slowly and carefully remount them on the handlebars. The grips were always tight, but a little of Mom's petroleum jelly made the job easier. The manufacturers must have known that alterations were going to take place because the holes in the grips were already manufactured into them—smart.

The longer the tassels, the better. The faster you pedaled, the more flutter you got, and the more your social position in the neighborhood increased. I always had a spare set of tassels in the garage just in case some mean kid decided to alter my handiwork.

The second alteration that any new bike owner had to install was a means to make the bike emanate as much noise as possible. We were too young to drive motorcycles, but they were everyone's dream. Therefore, we needed a bike that was a pretend motorcycle, at least noise-wise.

The noisemaker installation was an easy fix and only required items that you could readily find around the house. We didn't have a clothes dryer, so mom hung clothes on a line in the backyard to dry. Her basket of clothes pins was the perfect place to get the required fasteners. Mom and Dad loved to play cards, so there were lots of old decks of cards in the dining room drawers. I hoped that they wouldn't miss any of the aces or kings.

When the cards were properly attached to the frame of the bike, they would be in a position to interact with the spokes when the wheel turned. The flapping noise that the cards made increased in intensity the faster you pedaled. I always mounted multiple cards on both wheels, such that I had different sounds than the rest of the kids in the 'hood. The more noise, the better, but Dad didn't like it very much.

One problem with the noisemaker modification was that it was extremely destructive of the installed playing card. After a short time of being beat to a pulp by the wheel spokes, the card became ripped to pieces and no longer produced enough noise. However, there was an easy repair. I just installed queens and jacks, and then progressively moved on down the deck.

Christmas of my fifth-grade year turned out to be a special memory. Santa surprised me with a shiny new Schwinn. This was not just any Schwinn; it was the perfect shade of red, and more importantly, it had the tank mounted in the frame so that it resembled a motorcycle gas tank. I was clearly going to be a big deal in the neighborhood, so I set out to complete all the required alterations.

I was not disappointed because you could see the envy in my classmates' eyes as I would ride into the school bicycle parking spaces. I rode that bike every day, through some terrible rain and snow, just so I could continue being a big man in the schoolyard. When I got home, Mom would provide towels for me as I proudly wiped dirt and water from every inch of that beautiful red body.

There was no room in our small house to keep the bike at night, but we did have a tiny front porch. There was a roof over the porch, but it was not enclosed, so it didn't provide much protection from the weather. It was the only place I had, so the front porch was where my new status symbol spent its nights.

And then one very cold January night, all hell broke loose. It was about eleven thirty, and I was securely tucked in my bed. My bedroom was downstairs, in the unfinished basement, where Dad had constructed a plywood divider and door between me and the coal pile. With enough blankets, it was easy to stay warm. As I slept, dreaming of my new bike, the hell came.

Suddenly the plywood door flew off its poorly installed hinges, the lights came on, and a very loud voice shouted, "Where is your bike?" Dad always inspected the front porch when he got home.

I was disoriented, and terrified, but I was thinking fast, and I knew immediately what I had done. I also knew from experience that I'd better answer Dad quickly. I sat up in bed and said, "I left it at school." I also knew better than to say "I think"—Dad required preciseness in answers.

I must have gotten distracted playing after school and just walked home with my friends. Dad had always preached "focus," and I obviously had not. Recovery was the name of the game now, and recovery was going to be painful.

At high volume, Dad said, "Go get it." The outside temperature was in the low teens as I flew out the front door, into the night, heading south down F Street toward Central Ward Elementary. The distance was only about six blocks, and I was covering it fast, when I suddenly had a sinking feeling. What if the bike is not there? The outcome was too gruesome to think about, so as I rounded the last street corner, I held my breath.

There in the dark night, covered in new-fallen snow, was my red freedom ride. I quickly checked that all the parts were in place, jumped on, and pedaled like crazy, back up F Street.

I parked my ride in its place on the porch and then slunk through the house to my bedroom in the basement. Dad didn't say a word, and Mom just watched.

I know I wasn't supposed to see it, but there was a single set of car lights that slowly tracked my every movement during this cold event. When I arrived home, Dad was just putting the car back in the garage. He wanted me to learn a lesson, but he also wanted me to be OK.

I learned a lot about paying attention to detail and the need to "focus" that night. I never lost my bike again, and focus has helped me through many difficult adult situations.

## CHAPTER 13

**Hide the Beer**

––––––––––

My maternal grandparents were not what you would describe as party animals. In fact, teetotalers is a much better description of their way of life. My grandfather did smoke—and it killed him—but I doubt if he ever drank any liquor. And I'm absolutely positive that my grandmother never ever even held a drink in her hands. They did not preach their position or try to make other folks uncomfortable, but it was clear where they stood on the issue.

From my observations, it was also clear that they had attempted to instill the sobriety form of life in their children. I would say that they were about 50 percent successful.

My dad had one sister, and she and her husband appeared to follow the nondrinking example that had been set forward by Grandpa and Grandma. Conversely, my mom and dad had decided to travel a different road in life—one of fun. Mom and Dad were not heavy drinkers, but they did love a party, and they had many friends who traveled that same highway of entertainment.

Every Friday and Saturday night was an opportunity to have a shindig at someone's house. Sometimes the party would move from house to house, as the supplies ran low in one place. Those were the days of the "Tom Collins"—Old Crow bourbon—"Manhattans" and "Whiskey Sours," so your pantry needed to have a proper supply of the correct ingredients. I believe that there were also episodes of folks dancing on tables with lampshades on their heads. My mom was probably pretty good at that.

Grandma and Grandpa lived only about a block from our house, so it was convenient for Grandma to babysit me while Mom and Dad were out having fun. I really didn't like this arrangement much because it went on well after I was old enough to take care of myself. At least I thought so. However, it did set up a system where Mom and Dad had to come home in good shape or risk the fact that Grandma would find them out.

The direct path between my grandparent's house and our house was to come up the alleyway. The houses were so close together that you could see my grandparent's house from our kitchen window. Being able to observe Grandma's coming and goings turned out to be a significant intelligence advantage for my parents as they attempted to hide their fun-loving ways.

I was well into my high school days before we got a television, but it was just as well because there were very few stations that you could actually receive. Most of the channels were just a blurry, snowy mess, with dark figures moving around. You assumed that the figures were humans, and they were doing something important, but you didn't know what you were watching.

Dad loved to sit in front of the television, drink a beer, and watch what he thought was a football game. After a few years, the reception got better and he could actually identify the teams.

Mom was always in the kitchen—always. Therefore, she was assigned the additional duty of lookout. If Mom noted Grandma leaving her house and heading up the alleyway toward our house, she sounded the alarm. Actually, there was no alarm involved, but she did shout "Johnny, here she comes—hide the beer."

As Grandma entered through the back door and arrived in the kitchen, Dad would casually reach around his rocker and put the beer behind the chair. After Grandma completed her business with Mom, usually a cooking issue, she would come into the living room, sit down, and talk to Dad and me for a while. All the time, the beer was warming behind the chair.

With her mission complete, Grandma would go back down the alley, and Dad would retrieve his beer. As a kid, I watched this melodrama play out on many occasions, and I wondered if Grandma ever knew.

As a postscript, much later in life, I was home on leave, drinking beer and watching television with my dad when he was seventy-five years old. Suddenly, the alarm went off: "Johnny, here she comes—hide the beer." I couldn't believe my ears. Dad said, "Hide the beer," and I said, "I'm not doing that." He said, "You need to hide the beer." I did not hide the beer, but he did.

Grandma came into the living room, and Dad and I had a nice long talk with her as I drank my beer and Dad's got warm behind the chair. I guess you never get too old to want to please your mother.

I'm glad that my mom and dad took the highway of fun because that is the one that I traveled, and I would have hated to disappoint them.

## CHAPTER 14

## Don't Shoot the Dog

———

I loved to hunt, and at times during my childhood, it was a daily occurrence. If I was able to pull myself out of bed early enough on a cold morning, I could bag several rabbits or squirrels before it was time to head for school. If I misplanned my arrival back home from a hunt, there would not be enough time for me to clean the kill, and Mom would have to do it. I knew she didn't like that very much, but good-old Mom never complained.

I got my first gun before I was ten years old, and my grandpa took it upon himself to give me a few hunting lessons. From the beginning, it was clear that gun safety was not the issue. He gave me credit for having common sense. What he wanted was to make sure that whatever I brought home was edible. For example, there are certain times of year that you just don't eat wild rabbit. His instructions were that rabbit was not to be killed until after the first frost. When I asked the dumb question "Why," his answer was a swift theory-to-practice lesson. He shot the first unfortunate bunny we happened on and said, "Watch this." It was July. Using his trusty knife, he peeled back the fur from the rabbit's belly. I was stunned. There were many vivid sores and red places all over the rabbit body that apparently healed up in the cold months. To this very day, I cannot eat rabbit unless I know when it died.

Grandpa also insisted that I only hunt squirrel with a rifle and not a shotgun, and he would critique my kill each time I came home. If I had a squirrel that was not shot in the head, I was going to get an earful. His position was that squirrels are so small, if you shoot them with a shotgun or hit them any place on the body, you are ruining the meat. You had to be a good shot.

Watching the Saturday matinees and seeing the Indians and frontiersmen cleaning their game provided me with an idea. I noted that in addition to preparing the game for food, they used the hides of the critters for various pieces of clothing. It was my belief that if they could do that, so could I. Therefore, once, when I had time to do the cleaning myself, I carefully removed the pelt before any butchering process began. Mom got the meat and promptly started soaking the carcass in salt water because she believed that the gamey taste needed to be removed from the meat before cooking. It seemed to work because everybody ate what was served.

I wasn't big on using an encyclopedia, so I had no real idea of how to go about preparing and preserving the hide. I'd seen the Indians scraping the fatty tissue from the inside of the fur, so that is where I started. A search of Grandpa's carpenter tools produced instruments that would have to suffice as scrapers. The tools worked pretty well, but doing the scraping took a long time, even with a small rabbit pelt. I guess when you live on the frontier and can't buy clothes, you need to have a lot of tenacity.

When I thought I had scraped long enough, it was time to move on to the next step. Even though I had worked hard, the inside of the pelt was still pretty messy and bloody. My movie heroes dried the mess with salt, so off to Mom's kitchen I went. Again, Mom was not happy when I went to the basement with a year's supply of Morton's. But she didn't say anything. She liked me to experiment, as long as I didn't damage the house.

Another visit to the tool chest produced some nails and a piece of lumber that I could lie flat on the basement floor. I carefully stretched and nailed the pelt in place for drying. Then I spent the next few hours rubbing salt in every nook and cranny of the hide. I admired my work, but this job had been smellier than I anticipated, so I made a beeline to wash my hands.

The drying process took about a week, but the smell got worse, and this time Mom did complain. I had to move my potential fur gloves to the garage

The pelts were as stiff as a board when the drying process was complete, but I was bound and determined to make clothing from my work. There must have been a way to make them softer, but again, the research escaped me. After strenuous pelt bending and some difficult sewing with fishing line, I had furry mittens. Making glove fingers was too hard, and I decided to buy my future clothes in a store.

Hunting with friends was always more fun than walking the fields alone. It gave you a chance to discuss the issues of the day, and of course there was the friendly competition of who could kill the most game. When we got old enough to drive, we would take turns at the wheel in order to save gas money.

Driving also gave us the opportunity to cover more territory as we looked for the most productive hunting spots.

Gun safety was not something that we worried about. Oh, we knew it was important and it was carefully observed, but it was something that had been bred into us all our life. We all had had our own guns since our early youth, and our parents and grandparents had insisted on safety compliance. However, on one duck hunting occasion, I had a close call.

Fall months were the perfect time to hunt ducks. But water for the fowl to land on was scarce. Farm ponds were small and usually a fair distance from the roads. This made it difficult to see from the car if any ducks were present, and then you had to sneak up on them by crawling across a long, flat field. Finding a good duck hunting location was hard, but there was one prime location, some twenty to thirty miles from town, that we would visit periodically.

The water in this location was very shallow, much like a marsh, and it covered large areas of the surrounding fields. It was such a good duck hunting property that all of it was rented out for the season to rich folks from Lincoln and Omaha. At least I think they were rich. In any case, no one else was supposed to hunt there. Steve and I decided that the rich guys didn't hunt on weekdays, so it would be OK to poach a few ducks.

We slunk into the field and took up positions around a marshy area. I was on one side of the marsh and Steve was on the other side, straight across from me. We were only about thirty yards apart, but both of us were hunkered down and couldn't see each other. We waited and waited, and all along I kept expecting the law to show up before the ducks did.

Eventually I saw a lone duck headed into the pond. It was a teal, a very small duck, but a very fast flyer. He was all alone, but he was a target, and we hadn't had any other activity.

As ducks will do, just as they're landing they "brake" or flare their wings so they can land softly. Just as the teal flared, Steve and I both rose up at the same time and fired. The duck was directly between us, so we were also both in each other's line of fire.

The duck went down, but at the same time I saw Steve throw his hands in the air, scream, spin around, and fall face down in the marsh. I was sure I had killed my friend. I charged across the knee-deep water to find Steve lying in the weeds, laughing. I did not think it was funny. He had been hit but only by a couple of buckshot, doing no damage. All of us kids had taken a few buckshot from time to time, so it was no big deal, but it scared the hell out of me.

I was ready to go home for the day. At least the sheriff didn't get us.

The area around Fairbury is relatively flat land, with few trees, but there were numerous hedgerows and gullies that passed between grainfields. These places are the best for hunting, and Jefferson County was famous for its pheasant and quail population

I guess there were "no hunting" rules for fields, like there were for ponds, but we didn't pay much attention. Some farmers would have their land "posted" for no hunting, but it was hard to pass up a good gully that was next to a wheat or cornfield. Especially if you had a feeling that the birds were in there.

I know at times farmers would see us working our way down an off-limits treeline, but they never said anything, so we just kept doing it. Until one day!

With our twelve-gauge shotguns at the ready, I was with Steve and Steve's wonderful hunting dog, working our way along a strip of land that was bordered on one side by a grassy ditch and on the other by a newly picked cornfield. I could just feel that this place was full of pheasants, so we were walking slowly while we kicked piles of clumped grass. The dog was walking in a partial crouch as she sniffed the ground, looking like she could go on point at any minute. Pheasants have a habit of hunkering down until you almost step on them before taking flight.

Sometimes you just need to kick them out of their hiding places. Their sudden flushing and flight can startle you if you are not prepared.

I have no recollection of whether the field was "posted," but the area we were walking in was only about a quarter of a mile from a farmhouse. However, we were always careful not to fire in the direction of any building, so this was not a problem.

Suddenly, in the distance, I saw a bib-overall-clad figure coming out of the farmyard in our direction. I alerted Steve. In the past we had farmers come out of their house and talk to us. Usually the discussion was about whether we were having any luck, and wishing us well, before going back in the house. However, this event looked different. This guy was waving a shotgun, and it didn't appear like he wanted to join us in the hunt.

We were frozen in place, just watching as the gun-toter got closer. As he approached, he started yelling that we should get off his land. I, for one, was more than happy to comply with the orders being issued, but he just kept coming. When he was about thirty yards away, he pointed the twelve gauge in our direction and fired a warning shot over our heads. I heard a yelp as the dog started running. The shooter just yelled, "Now get," spun around, and walked swiftly back to his house. I know he was just trying to scare us, but we would have left without the expenditure of ammunition. It just happened so fast.

We ran to the car as fast as we could, where we found the dog cowering behind a tire. A quick inspection of the canine revealed no injury, but we suspected that one of the buckshot just grazed him, though we couldn't confirm. I was scared and ready to go home, but Steve was livid. He kept yelling that "the SOB shot my dog."

Steve was driving that day, so when I piled in the car, I assumed that we were headed for town. I was wrong. At high speed Steve spun the car around in the gravel road and headed for the farmhouse. I remember thinking, *Crap*. Steve was mad. We entered the farmyard at equally high speed and crossed the area between the house and the barn before Steve slammed on the brakes. I did not know what was going to happen, but I knew it was going to be ugly

When Steve jumped out of the car and grabbed his shotgun from the back seat, I was afraid he was going to shoot the farmer. Instead, he headed for the smaller building near the barn—the henhouse.

He violently kicked open the door of the hen house and rapidly pumped three twelve-gauge number four shot rounds into the henhouse interior. All the time he was screaming, "Don't shoot the dog." I know he would have fired more rounds if he could, but that was all of the weapon's capacity. I never saw any chicken deaths, but I know there must have been some—maybe many.

Steve got back in the car, very leisurely, as if he felt like his work was done here. As we slowly started to pull out of the farmyard, Steve rolled down the window and shouted one last time—"Don't shoot the dog." The farmer never came out of the house, and nothing was ever heard about the episode. Lucky for us.

We never hunted in that part of the county again.

## CHAPTER 15

## And Then There Was Rod

---

Just as it is with adults, the world is full of good kids and bad kids, kids with black clouds over their head, kids that take too long to grow up, and others just having so much fun that they don't care which category they fit into. Rod didn't fit neatly into any of these little niches because he was a good kid that loved pulling the most outrageous pranks, sometimes involving himself in such hair-brained schemes that he constantly found himself on the police usual suspect list every time something unusual happened. Rod was not the kind of person who woke up in the morning and decided that he was going out and break the law. However, he was the kind of person who took great pride in thinking up an activity that would shock the rest of the town. He knew that most of his plans were too good not to carry out the deed, irrespective of the possible legal consequences. I doubt that he ever used the term itself, but he was a master of shock.

At times Rod would just throw out an outrageous idea. Something that would cause the hair on people's necks to rise up. Then he would just step back and see which one of his buddies would snap at the bait and go try it. Besides being the master of shock, Rod was an instigator.

A postscript is necessary before enlightening the reader with a few of Rod's exploits. It was touch and go during the dustup of some events, but Rod never spent a day in jail. Later in life he became a very successful businessman, proving that it is not how you start but how you finish that counts.

Now, where was I—oh, yes, Rod as a teenager.

Rod was one of those kids that came in from a one-room country school to spend his high school days in the city. He was an above-average student, participated in a fine manner on athletic teams, and was involved in a grand assortment of school activities. I can't think of one soul that didn't like Rod.

He grew up on a farm near Gladstone, a small town just west of Fairbury. Gladstone had been established back in 1886 at the end of a Chicago, Kansas and Nebraska Railway spur, but that spur didn't exist when Rod lived there. We were fond of teasing Rod about the name Gladstone by calling it "Laughing Pebble" or "Happy Rock," but he didn't seem to mind. Even though the town was originally named for a United Kingdom prime minister, it had never grown. Gladstone had one store, one car garage (that belonged to Rod's dad), a post office, and a grain elevator. There were only a handful of houses and two churches, the West Gladstone Church and the East Gladstone Church. I never understood why such a small town, with only forty-five residents, needed two churches. Rod once told me that it was because the town had two levels of sinners. And, of course, why did they need a direction in their name but no denomination? Seemed stupid to me.

If the entire population of the town went to church, there might be fifteen people total in both congregations. Gladstone was pretty small. In fact, the only other classmate who had come from Gladstone was Dick, and Dick had some of the same shock tendencies as Rod, but not nearly as dramatic. Perhaps there was something in the Gladstone water.

Another postscript—Dick went on to be the successful superintendent of a large school system, and I always had to smile when I thought of him in that position. I could just picture some kid trying to convince Dick of an untruth or that he hadn't committed a misdeed. Dick knew every trick in the book.

Dick's partner in life, his wife, is one lucky person because she almost ended up with Rod. Seems that while double dating, Dick was not satisfied that his date met his standards. After informing Rod of the fact, Rod said, "Here, take mine," so Dick did. Must have worked out because Dick now has more kids, grandkids, and great-grandkids than the entire population of Gladstone. Rod takes credit for all of Dick's success.

Rod was not what you would call a good-looking dude, and he certainly was not physically imposing. However, he always had a much newer and nicer car than the rest of the guys, so the girls liked to ride around town with him as their designated driver. His gray Chevy had a few years on it, but the engine was powerful and almost like new. When Rod started high school, he needed a car so he could make the eight-mile drive from Gladstone. His dad purchased the low-mileage Chevy from the West Gladstone Church minister, and the preacher man had not been out of Gladstone that much.

You didn't see Rod on many dates, and he never went out with any of the cheerleaders, but all the "in" girls liked to just sit in Rod's wheels and eat their lunch during the school noon hour. It was obvious where all the girls were when you saw most of the football team leaning in the windows of Rod's car, just so they could converse with their girlfriends. However, squiring ladies around town was not the only pasttime that Rod found for his car.

Rod was famous for taking on all comers when it involved driving fast, while executing unimaginable turns. Bets would be placed as the competition would start on a hard-top highway about a half mile from a ninety-degree turn onto a loose-gravel road. The winner was the person who could make that turn, at the highest speed, without losing control or rolling the car over. When the engine in that polished Chevy started to roar down the highway toward the turn, you were sure that you were about to watch Rod die. As the car entered that ninety-degree turn at over fifty miles per hour, the car's rear end would slide to the left, almost passing the front end, while dirt and gravel and dust were thrown up in an opaque cloud. It was hard to see, but part of the car would disappear down the side of the ditch before you heard the roar of acceleration, and the car would again appear as it fishtailed down the gravel road.

After the copious cheering, laughter, and thankfulness for not observing something awful, Rod would announce that he was dissatisfied because the speed was too low, and he was going to do it again. Rod never lost any bets at these events.

When Rod got bored, there was always the trip to the south side of town where the state Highway 15 viaduct passed over the Rock Island Railroad tracks. Rod had discovered a roughly maintained road, under the viaduct, running parallel to the tracks. Railroad personnel used the road for track access and when conducting rail maintenance. Rod quickly realized that this road also gave him access to the very steep incline, up the side of the viaduct. He just couldn't pass up an opportunity to again test his driving skills. Even those of us who had taken a few trigonometry classes never actually calculated the exact incline of that hill, but I'm betting that it was at least sixty degrees. But the exact incline of that hill was not important to Rod because he just needed it to be enough for him to perform his next death-defying feat.

The access road was not very long, but again, it didn't matter. The Chevy would be backed away from the hill, and Rod would give it enough speed to make it almost to the highway guardrail at the top of the incline. With enough speed, getting to the top was easy, but that was not what Rod was attempting to accomplish. As the car started up that almost vertical incline, the front wheels of the car would start to come off the ground, even as the car continued to climb. Nobody could challenge Rod in how long that car would stand straight up in the air on its rear wheels before the courage ran out and he would let out on the clutch. Hopefully, the car would slam down on its front tires and roll backward down the hill. There were many nights that we expected to see that Chevy with its wheels sticking straight up in the air, and Rod somewhere inside, but it never happened.

As already established, Friday nights were very special from a high school sports night perspective, and it's always good to be playing on the home field or court. This is especially the case when you are about to do combat with one of your school's archrivals. Beatrice, a town that was at least four times the size of Fairbury, was located twenty-nine miles east-northeast down Highway 136. We considered the "Orange Men" to be our most fierce rival.

Rod, however, had decided that it didn't matter whether we won or lost the competition, our team, the Jeffs, should send the visiting team home with a surprise.

The planning phase for Rod's next great adventure started with a reconnaissance trip down the full twenty-nine miles of state Highway 136. He needed to map out the best location for his proposed interaction. At night, Highway 136 was a dark two-lane blacktop, with very little traffic. There was only one small town in the entire twenty-nine mile stretch, and it could be passed through at the speed limit. Much of the highway had originally run parallel to a railroad bed. The highway bed had been built so that in many places there were slightly inclined grassy shoulders that rolled away from the road and down to a shallow ditch. After finding several acceptable locations along the highway, Rod was ready to roll. However, even he knew that this operation was not without danger to himself and others. A few beers would restore his lost courage

Rod and a few trusted accomplices waited in the school parking lot that night after the game. They watched as the visiting team departed the gymnasium and, one by one, loaded up in the yellow school bus for their one-hour trip home. As the bus traveled up K Street and turned right onto Highway 136, the gray Chevy was only a few blocks behind, well within visual range. Once the bus was on the highway and the city lights were left behind, the dark night set the stage. Usually you can travel a long way on

136 without seeing many cars, and that night was no different. Therefore, it was no problem for Rod and his crew to follow a few hundred yards behind the bus and not lose contact, even though Rod's car lights were turned off.

As the bus and the Chevy approached one of Rod's predesignated sites, it was time to put the plan into action. After a couple of final sips of beer, Rod accelerated the Chevy to only a few feet from the bus's rear bumper. With the Chevy lights out and the car tucked in so close to the bus, there was no way the bus driver could tell that Rod was on his tail. The perfect grassy road shoulder approached. Rod turned to the right onto the road shoulder and stomped on the accelerator as he drove next to the moving bus. Just as the Chevy pulled even with the front of the bus, Rod turned on the car's lights and leaned on the horn, causing the poor bus driver to swerve hard to the left, almost losing control. It's unverified, but my guess is that the bus driver might have lost control of a bodily function. Rod then turned the lights off again, slowed the car down, and made a turn in the highway, heading back to town, as the bus was last seen zigzagging toward home.

Rod was known for doing things that sometimes put himself in danger, but this could have turned out terribly if that busload of students had crashed, and

I think Rod knew it. Even though there were other Rod shock events on the horizon, we never again saw one that put others in immediate danger.

The authorities knew that Rod was always up to something, so they continually had him on their usual suspects list, even when he was innocent. One occurrence of that was the night that Dennis—not me, a third Dennis—decided that it might be amusing to shoot himself.

The party had started in a farm pasture that was owned by Dick's parents, and it was so far out in the boonies that nobody was bothered by the noise and the excessive drinking. When a party is held in a pasture, the drunks only have to worry about going facedown in a cow pie or drowning in a horse watering tank. Rod had been to the party earlier in the evening but left because he was scheduled to get up in the morning and drive to Colorado for a summer job. One of the few times that Rod showed the proper discretion. But in the end he would still wind up in trouble.

Dennis was an interesting kid who was a year ahead of me in high school. He was never at the head of his class, but he had an amazing capacity to read fast and absorb copious amounts of knowledge. I didn't know what it meant at the time, but the news articles that had been written about him said that

234

he had a photographic memory. He could start and finish a book before I could read the title, and, therefore, he got bored if he wasn't kept busy.

The party was in full swing, so alcohol probably had something to do with the outcome. About two in the morning, Dennis got bored and decided that some excitement was needed. He announced that with a little financial inducement, he would be willing to shoot himself. As the cheering commenced, money started to appear on the top of an empty beer case. When the total reached about ten dollars, Dennis declared that would be enough, and the search for a gun commenced. The search did not take long because every kid in the county carried a rifle in their car, just in case there was time for hunting on the way home from school. Dick's .22-caliber rifle was quickly retrieved from behind the front seat of his car and delivered to the waiting hands of Dennis.

Everyone just assumed that the gun was loaded because guns were rarely unloaded, so once Dennis had the gun in hand, the deed was very quickly done. Without explanation or comment, he placed the muzzle of the weapon against his left shoulder, just above his heart, and pulled the trigger. Small-caliber weapons usually don't make much noise when fired, but on this night the exploding chamber noise seemed to be deafening. Nobody moved or said a word until Dennis dropped the weapon and proceeded to the nearby cooler to get another beer. The bullet had made a small hole going in and out and there was some, but not an inordinate amount, of blood, so he was ready to continue the party.

Before the night was over, even though his inebriated friends had "field dressed" him in the pasture, it was decided that Dennis should probably see a doctor. That is where Rod's problems started, even though he had left the party early and was now at home in bed.

The next morning, as planned, Rod headed west to Colorado to start a new summer job. Also early in the morning, after being alerted by the doctor, the police were interrogating Dennis about the details of the shooting and who else was present at the party. It didn't surprise the authorities when Rod's name came up because Rod was always on the usual suspects list.

The sheriff and his deputy arrived at Rod's parent's house, with guns drawn, to arrest him as an accomplice to a shooting. There was also this little fact that Rod was already on probation for other assorted previous events and was not supposed to be drinking, associating with criminals, around firearms, or staying out late at night. The sheriff was ready to throw the book at him. However, when the sheriff found out that Rod was on his way out of the state, it got even worse because he was not supposed to leave the county.

I'm not sure that Rod ever knew how the event got worked out, but his probation officer and the county judge, Bob's dad, figured some way to keep him out of jail. I guess they rationalized that even though he had broken every rule of his probation, he had not been present at the shooting. It is good to have friends in high places, especially if you are the master of shock

Leaving some parties early was just out of the question because of the camaraderie and, of course, the quantity of beer present. Additionally, parties held in someone's remote farm field were even better because there was a reasonable chance that there would be no interruptions by the sheriff. Even driving home could be avoided if you didn't mind sleeping in a haystack.

Rod did not miss many of the best events, and actually was the organizer of most. His reputation for the consumption of alcohol was legendary, but you rarely saw him in a drunken state. He always had a happy personality, but after a few beers, his dry sense of humor was world-class, and everyone loved being around him.

One of the nights that Rod did succumb to the alcohol in a large amount of beer has been documented as taking place in Connie's dad's pasture. To this day, I'm not sure if he was really drunk or just being his old playful self by trying to shock the rest of the partygoers. That being said, he started talking about the fact that he might have consumed too much and, for some reason, he was having trouble breathing. At first, drinking too much and not being able to breath didn't register with a bunch of teenagers as something they should worry themselves about. However, after a while it was determined that Rod really did need assistance, so a hasty meeting was called to plan a remedy. Rod even took part in the meeting, where it was decided that we needed a way to force large amounts of air down Rod's throat. Connie's mother's fan was discussed but dismissed because of insufficient air flow

As usual, with young folks who have drunk too much liquor, the final decision on how to save Rod's life involved the employment of an automobile. Cars in the 1950s were less sleek, with more defined bumpers and fenders that were perfect for sitting on when no other seats were available. At parties, or just on a street corner, you would find young folks chatting while lounging on their vehicle's fender.

It was determined that there was no better way to force air into Rod's lungs than to prop him up on the fender of a 1949 Chevy and drive down a gravel country road at high speed. Rod, being a car guy, agreed that this might work. There was concern that the plan might fail if Rod didn't hold his mouth open wide enough to allow the flow of air. So an additional parameter was added to the experiment. The girls rounded up some toothpicks and also found some old popsicle sticks. Along with some tape, the sticks were perfect for holding Rod's mouth and eyes open. He looked a little grotesque as the boys mounted him on the left car fender and gave him last-minute instructions to hang on,

By this time everyone at the party was cheering as the Chevy flat-head six-cylinder engine was started and the car started to roll down the gravel road. It was a very dark night, but the full load of riders could plainly see Rod, framed by the headlights, bouncing on the fender as the car reached forty miles an hour. Teens were hanging out the windows, encouraging him to hold on and asking him how he was doing, when an unplanned event took place

On country roads you can never predict what kind of wild animals you might see, especially darting out of the darkness. Tonight it would be a large jackrabbit. Rabbits in Nebraska are plentiful and are usually something that you don't mind hitting. However, as the rabbit appeared in the headlights, the driver instinctively slammed on the brakes. Rod was last seen being jettisoned from the fender, with arms outstretched in superman form, flying down the center of the road at about five feet off the ground. He didn't hit the gravel road until he had flown completely beyond the illumination of the car's lights, and the landing was not a pretty thing to watch.

Rod skipped and rolled in the gravel road several times, so by the time the entourage reached his position, he was sitting up in a bloody mess. The force of the sand had ripped most of his clothes into a tatter, and his body looked like the end result was going to be a five-foot-seven-inch-tall scab. However, as usual, Rod was smiling through his bloody teeth. When it was determined that Rod had again escaped death, it was time to return to the party, but Rod spent the rest of the night in a back bedroom. My guess is that he suffered. Continuing the party was important, and after all, Rod was breathing much better than he had before the ride, so the operation had obviously been a success.

Even though Rod was always present on the police most suspected list, it did not deter him from finding ways to elevate his position on that list. The police department was very small, with only one or two cars and the same number of officers, so they were an easy target for a smart kid like Rod. Even though Rod knew that he was in the crosshairs of the authorities, he took this notoriety as a manhood challenge to outwit the men in blue.

The police station was right in the middle of downtown, and the main street passed just fifteen feet from the station's front door. Usually the town was very quiet, so after a routine security drive around the entire town, which you could do in about twenty minutes, the officers would return to the station for a much-needed cup of coffee. Rod had watched this routine over a period of time and decided that some night it might be fun to confuse the local fuzz.

His plan was to wait around the corner from the police station until the patrolling officer exited his car and entered the station for a pee and coffee break. Rod was joined by a few of his running mates in their lookout position, so moral support for this episode was not lacking. There had been some earlier beer drinking to bolster the egos, so with the addition of the pressure not to let his friends down, the plot was put into action

Rod casually walked around the corner and toward the empty police cruiser that was parked at the curb, with its engine still running. While passing the station, he peered in the window to ensure that the officer was still in the bathroom. From that point on, it was easy. Just back the car out of the parking area and proceed down the street to the cruiser's next parking space.

All along, the plan had been to simply tweak the police by moving the car about half a block, believing that the officers were so dumb that they would think they had misplaced the vehicle. However, after Rod's cohorts met him at the new parking area with loud congratulations, he knew that this thing was going so well that it must continue. All hands agreed, and everyone quickly piled into the cruiser as Rod sped out toward the south end of town.

Rod had always wanted to drink beer while sitting in a police car, so that is what the group did over the next couple of hours as they cruised around Jefferson County. As the night wore on and the beer ran out, Rod started thinking about how he was going end this fun. His friends were too drunk to be any help in decision making, so all on his own he came up with a plan that in the ensuing days would not be understood by his friends, the police, and especially the county judge.

After parking the car on a remote hill side, Rod ushered the group out of the vehicle, to a safe distance away from the cruiser. He then retrieved the official issue twelve-gauge shotgun from behind the seat and loaded it with a full magazine of ammunition. Rod was a smart kid, so his thinking must have been clouded with alcohol because he had decided that perhaps the authorities would not recognize the cruiser if it had a slight face-lift. Anyway, how would they know he was involved in the first place? Those being his last thoughts, and to the cheers of the onlookers, he raised the weapon and pumped six rounds into the defenseless car.

The next morning, with drawn pistols, the authorities again appeared on Rod's front porch. From this time on, history is a little fuzzy. There was a lot of high-powered meetings involving every lawyer in town, and, of course, Judge Sam. In the end they must have decided that Rod was worth saving. After quite a bit of financial restitution, aggressive counseling, and more probation, Rod lived to shock another day.

I often think about how boring my childhood would have been without a Rod in my life.

## CHAPTER 16

## Harold

———————

Entering junior high school was a very big deal when I was growing up. For the first time in my academic career, I was not housed, schooled, and classified as a grade school student. My classrooms were now in the high school building, and I learned the routine of changing classrooms and teachers every hour. I also learned very quickly that those same teachers were going to expect a lot more of me in the area of grades. Being a seventh and eighth grader was a huge social step in my growing-up process.

In addition to the changed academic environment, junior high was the first time in my life where there were actually organized sports teams. Teams with coaches, uniforms, and scheduled competition with surrounding towns. Looking back now, it was probably silly, but to me, this was more important than classrooms and grades. I loved the thought of competition, and even though I was very small in weight and stature, my dad had convinced me that I could defeat anyone, at any time—a theory that would be tested many times, and many times I failed to live up to my own and my dad's expectations.

With this in mind, you can understand how excited I was when, in August, the Fairbury *Daily News* announced that during the following week, the school would be checking out football practice uniforms. This was two weeks before school was to start, but a great time for the coaches to hold two-a- day practices and to see what prospective athletes had to offer.

The following Monday morning I was standing at the door of the gymnasium, even before it was scheduled to open. The equipment room for the junior high was a very small room at one end of the old basketball court. When I arrived that morning, I was not only the first person there that day, I was the only person.

I had no idea that the person I would meet that day was going to have such a major impact on the rest of my teenage days. As I stepped into that equipment room, I met Harold for the very first time. I knew he was the coach, so I tried to look taller and bigger and tougher than a glance at my eighty-five-pound body would indicate. He asked me what I wanted, and I remember thinking that was a dumb question because I wouldn't be there unless I wanted to check out a uniform and try out for the team. But the thing that remains with me till this very day was the smile that crept across his face.

Harold kept smiling and said that he was looking for an equipment manager and that I might fit the bill. Besides, he explained, he did not have a uniform that was small enough for me. I was as stunned and hurt as a thirteen-year-old can be. Plus, there was no way that I was going home to tell my dad that I wasn't big enough to play football.

I had been trained to never talk back to adults, but this was a special circumstance, so Harold got my best blast. Actually, it wasn't a blast, but I made it very clear that I was going to try out for the team. As I talked, Harold never stopped smiling. When I was done, he told me to come back tomorrow and he would see what he could do. I didn't tell my dad what happened, and I didn't sleep much that night.

The next day I again arrived early at the gym to find Harold still smiling. As I walked in, he threw a pair of football pants at me and told me to try them on. As football fans know, hip pads are a separate piece of equipment that is worn under the pants, but not in this case. These pants must have been bought at a child's store because the hip pads were sewn into the beltline. As I pulled those pants on, Harold asked if I could run fast. I told him that I was very quick, and as he continued to smile, he said, "You had better be." And thus, my athletic career began. Those pants were still too big, but I never complained. In fact, on game days the rest of the team would get entire sets of game-day uniforms, but not me. I received a game-day jersey, but I wore those same pants to practice and to games the entire year.

As the days of practice passed, it became obvious to the coach that I was fast and quick and hard to catch. He started using me as a punt and kickoff runback specialist, and my confidence grew. As the date of our first game approached, I found myself as the number two running back, behind an eighth grader named Barry. Barry was not only older and bigger than me, but he was also better than me. I didn't know Barry well, but I do remember that he was a year ahead of me in school, and that was significant.

Then one day Barry did not show up for practice. The word got around that Barry was sick, but I just assumed that he would soon be back on the field with the rest of us. After all, we all get sick once in a while. But Barry did not come back, at least for a long time.

I had never heard of the disease, but it seems that Barry had been stricken with leukemia, and he was very sick. When he did return to school, many months later, he was without one leg, as it had been amputated in an effort to save his life. This was a severe shock to my young intellect because it had never crossed my mind that anything like this would happen. We were young and invincible, and we were going to be great football players.

Barry took all this hardship much better than I would have. I recall that he used to play touch football with us after our church youth group meetings, and as usual, he was a very good player, despite the fact that he had a prosthetic leg. And then, Barry was gone again.

This time he did not come back. Within a short period of time he was gone from this world. Now my head was really spinning because death was just not something that happens to teenagers in Fairbury, Nebraska. I grew up a lot during that funeral.

I became the starting running back on a football team because the young man in the coffin got sick and died. That has always bothered me, and I think of the situation often. I'm sure that I didn't voice this position out loud, but ever since that day, I have known that it was important to live each day like it is the last. Barry's death really frightened me.

As in most small towns, coaches have a vast array of other responsibilities during the school year and beyond. Harold was also the basketball and track coach, as well as a teacher. Therefore, I saw a lot of him on a daily basis, but our relationship remained that of a coach to athlete and student until about the time that I entered high school. It was at that time that I was hired as a lifeguard at the city swimming pool, and Harold was the manager of the pool.

My guess is that when I first got hired as a guard, Harold had something to do with it. The pay chart for guards was controlled by the city council because we were legally city employees. So, Harold was probably also involved when, after two years, my salary went from fifty cents an hour to seventy-five cents. He made my employment enjoyable, and because he understood my financial situation, he looked out for me.

We always had four or five guards, but Harold would make sure that I got all the extra hours of work. The pool didn't open until one o'clock, but the morning hours were required to just get the dressing rooms and pool area cleaned up from the previous day's swimmers. I was the only guard that ever got that assignment, so I could log four hours before the other employees started. A financial bluebird!

I recognized and appreciated the fact that Harold treated me differently. He would pick me up every morning from my home and deliver me to the pool. He was always there at the pool with me, just tinkering, while I worked. But it also gave us time to talk. And we talked about everything, from school to politics, to growing up, to what I wanted to do with my life, and, of course, girls. He told me to be smart with my emotions—good advice.

Like a father figure, or a big brother, or just a good friend, he made it clear that I needed to keep my nose clean in everything that I did. I didn't think about it at the time, but Harold was only ten years older than me, and he was becoming like a big brother. It was during this time that I realized that other than my father, Harold was becoming the most important man in my life.

By the time I entered high school Harold had become the high school track coach and the assistant principal. This was perfect for me because it was just like having a good friend travel along with you as you journeyed through life. He was always tough on me, but always fair. When he didn't think I was working hard enough at practice, he was fond of yelling "Jones, if you had a wooden leg, you would be shit on a stick." At other times he would suggest that I was so slow that "I could run all day in a tub and never find the drain." Most of the time he was correct. I wasn't working hard enough.

The memory of some people sticks with you always, even when those people only cross your path in a fleeting fashion. There was one person in particular that could have ended my mission to "keep my nose clean." Let's just call him Larry for purposes of this storytelling. Larry had started out in the high school class ahead of me but had dropped out of school when he was a junior in order to join the Navy. Actually, Larry was in trouble a lot, so I'm not sure he dropped out of school or was ordered by the law to join the Navy. Whatever the circumstances, Larry was only gone for about a year, and then he was back in town and assigned to my high school class. I have always suspected that even the Navy didn't want him, but that is just a guess.

To my knowledge, I had never had a discussion with Larry. But for some reason he decided that he did not like me. Strange things started to happen to my car. When I found the radio antenna broken off after a basketball game, I assumed the culprit was a disgruntled rival town fan. But then I found it broken off again, shortly after repair. I started to hear rumors that Larry was enjoying himself a lot when telling stories of the antenna-breaking escapades. I guess that at first I was just too chicken to confront him because first of all, I just wasn't sure, and second, he was much bigger than me.

Then came the time that he really tripped my anger latch. In those days nobody ever locked their car. It was just not necessary. We were a very trusting small-town population, so if someone wanted to do some internal damage to your car, it was an easy mark. Larry decided to take advantage of that trust one evening while I was at basketball practice. It was a bitter-cold Nebraska night when I started my car and turned on the heater. The heater exhaust in that 1949 Chevy was under the front seat, and when the hot air began to blow, the Limburger cheese that Larry had placed all over the underside of the seat began to stink. The more I thought about it, the madder I got.

By morning, in my head, I was about six feet tall and weighed 220 pounds—enough was enough. My school locker was on the third floor of the school, and I knew that Larry's was just down the hall. I had decided to wait until after school was over, when most of the students had cleared out, before I made my move. As it worked out, Larry had an extra enforced study period that day, so my timing worked out perfectly. He was just opening his locker door when I showed up alongside of him and slammed his door shut. He was startled, and I was trying to look as large as possible. I poked him in the chest and accused him of all the wrongdoings that had been going on. I ducked just in time to avoid his first swing.

The fight had been joined, and as we threw punches and rolled down the hall, it was obvious to me that this was not going to end well. We were entangled and both bleeding as we fell down the stairs to the landing between floors, and then around the corner and down the rest of the stairs to the second floor. When we came to rest at the bottom of the stairs, it put us right in front of the principal's office, but the fight continued. It must have been a great commotion because the next thing I remember was Harold pulling Larry and myself apart. I don't remember much of the next few seconds, but I know that Larry was dragged into the office and I was told to "get." I thought for sure I was in big trouble, but it must have been Harold to the rescue because Larry never bothered me again. The next day at basketball practice Harold simply said, "I told you to keep your nose clean," and that was the end of it

I have memories of many teachers, and most of these memories are very positive. In their own way, all of these teachers had a major impact on my young life. However, none can compare to the old coach, Harold.

## CHAPTER 17

## Carolyn Kay

——————

Early in my high school years, the pretty young daughter of a hardworking Jefferson County dryland farmer walked into my life and forever changed my outlook on boy-girl relationships. For the next several years, Carolyn Kay would be the source of every good memory that I possess from that time period. She taught me to trust, to believe, to dream, and to love. She was not only a wonderful girlfriend, she was, and remains, a very precious friend.

The beginning of freshman year is when the country kids come to school in town for the first time. Up until that point, these new students had spent the first eight years of their education in one-room schoolhouses around the county. These first few days were exciting as you met new friends and you discovered what big athletic farm boys you have as new teammates in the coming football season. Looking back, these new classmates added greatly to our class, in every conceivable area. They not only fit right in but they also assumed large leadership roles, all the way through our four years together.

I don't recall the first time that I met or even saw Carolyn Kay. Therefore, I'm sure that we did not have one of those "love-at-first-sight" encounters. What I do remember was that I began to notice her because she seemed to be involved in every school activity imaginable. To me, she was more sophisticated than the other girls, and I wasn't sure I was in her league. But what red-blooded American boy doesn't notice pretty girls who are in the pep club and then become cheerleaders? There is something special about your girlfriend on the sideline, cheering for you. Even when I knew that I wanted Carolyn Kay in my life, I'm not sure she knew that she was going to be my girlfriend. So, this was going to be a work in progress.

The place to be in the summertime was the public swimming pool. Every warm summer day would find all the young folks congregated there to socialize and get the world's greatest suntan. As a lifeguard I got to be with my friends all day and make a little money while doing it. As has been discussed, "a little money" is the operative phrase. Carolyn was generally part of the swimming pool crowd, so I saw her on most of Nebraska's hot, sunny summer days. There is something to be said about spending the day watching your swimsuit-clad girlfriend.

In the beginning she was too young to drive, but her mother would bring her to town to be with her friends at the pool. The term "raging hormones" is the only way to describe the excitement that I felt whenever I saw that new-model Buick enter the pool parking lot.

There was no one defining moment when we declared that we were "a thing" or "a couple." It just seemed to happen over time. We were enjoying what was happening in our lives, and our friends accepted us as a couple. I remember feeling very special because one of the school's prettiest girls cared about me.

With no computers or iPhones, the mode of written communication during those days was with a stubby pencil and a piece of notebook paper. Passing notes in or between classes was something that could get you in trouble with the administration very quickly, but it was something that was done all the time. If you didn't get a note from your significant other as you passed in the hall, you should be concerned that your relationship may be headed south.

The very best time to get a special note was just before you stepped onto the school bus headed for an athletic contest in a rival town. These notes were usually longer and more personal, and exalted you to do well in the contest. The phrase "I will be watching you and look forward to seeing you after the game" could cause shivers of joy as the bus chugged its way to the contest. Those days were much simpler than today for young folks. The notes never, or at least the notes I received, contained sexually explicit or suggestive wording. However, there was enough in the note to excite the mind with visions of what might happen on a future day.

Being with Carolyn Kay during those years exposed me to social opportunities that I could not have otherwise dreamed of. We were such a recognizable couple throughout the school that we were chosen as the king and queen of various events. Without her at my side, there is no way I could have enjoyed such notoriety. I was clearly smitten, and as far as I was concerned, the future was bright. Heck, even her folks liked me.

I doubt that many of my classmates would believe it, because I think I disguised it pretty well, but I was a very insecure young man throughout my high school days. I never felt like I was good enough at anything. As a result, I was probably the classic over-achiever. With Carolyn Kay in my life, I not only had a pretty girlfriend, but she opened doors for me that otherwise would not have been possible. Her presence instilled in me the confidence that I so much needed to be successful later in life.

Carolyn's older sister was married and lived a couple hundred miles away from Fairbury. On several occasions, when Carolyn and her family would travel to visit the sister, I would be asked to come along. To me, this was a signal that I was accepted by the entire clan, and it gave me a warm fuzzy feeling about our relationship. I still recall sitting in the backseat on those long trips and periodically sneaking a hand hold while receiving an understanding smile. All was well in my world.

At times her dad would employ me to work on the farm, which gave me additional time in Carolyn's life. My normal chore was putting in barbed-wire fence. Earl would leave me alone to dig holes and string fence, while periodically checking in on me during the day. You can do a lot of thinking when left alone to dig a series of holes. As I recall, he seemed to be impressed with my hole-digging ability, and I was eager to please. At noon and at evening mealtimes he would drive me back to the farmhouse where

Carolyn and her mother would have prepared plentiful meals. I know it sounds silly, but the thought of sitting at the kitchen table, across from the most special person in your life after completing a hard day's work, was an unbelievable happening. I was living a wonderful dream.

Labor Day of my sophomore year was a major turning point in my athletic career. It was two weeks before school was to start, but the football team was practicing two times a day, getting ready for the season. I remember that it was a hot day—a very hot day—and we were conducting one-on-one drills. With two tackling dummies spaced about eight feet apart, and a lineman positioned on one side of the opening between the dummies, a running back would run through the opening in an attempt to get past the tackler. I had successfully completed the drill several times, and now it was my turn again. As discussed on multiple occasions, I was very small in size, but my quickness had been a problem for the potential tacklers. This time I drew an ultra-large senior named Delvin. As I hit the hole, Delvin unloaded on me, but usually this was not a problem because I'd just spin out of his grasp and embarrass him. This time as I spun, my cleats stuck in the ground and my leg did not spin with me. When Delvin climbed off, my knee and leg were facing the wrong direction.

Even I knew that I was finished for the season, and a few days later I underwent knee surgery.

This kind of surgery was not possible in Fairbury, so it was conducted in Lincoln at St. Elizabeth's Hospital—which now is named CHI Health St. Elizabeth and has expanded beyond the hospital I knew. I remember that the doctor's name was Stone and that he was the orthopedic doctor for the University of Nebraska football team—I was in good hands. When I woke up from surgery, there was Carolyn Kay. My mom and dad had driven to Lincoln to be with me, and they had been thoughtful enough to bring her along. It is impossible to explain how much this meant to me—not only that they would ask her, but that Carolyn would want to be there. To this very day, I still have the small gift that she brought me. It was an ugly little creature called a "worry bird," with a note about how much she cared for me. She made this the best surgery that I ever had!

The Denny and Carolyn Kay relationship continued to accelerate throughout our sophomore and junior year, and frankly, I was convinced that it would never end. We spent every possible moment together.

All generations of young lovers have their own version of "lover's lane," and we were no different. In the 1950s Nebraska kids would spend dark evenings in their cars, parked along a country road. The radio would be tuned to KOMA out of Oklahoma City, which, because of atmospheric conditions in the Midwest, you could only get at night. The tunes of the early rock-and-roll years would play as couples would explore each other. Kids of today will chuckle at the next revelation, but nothing of an absolute sexual nature ever happened, at least not with me and Carolyn Kay. I recall enormous frustration at the time, but today I rejoice in this fact. I'm not sure the lifetime friendship that the two of us have enjoyed would have existed if sex had been involved. That being said, some exploring seemed acceptable. How else would I find out that a Kleenex-filled bra makes a girl feel much more mature?

Of course, there were also the visible signs of affection that were necessary to advertise to the world that a relationship existed. As a cheerleader, Carolyn Kay needed to wear my letter jacket to emphasize to opposing teams that she had a man in the fight. I don't recall seeing that jacket after graduation, so she may still have it. The distribution of class rings at the end of our junior year was a big event. The event became an even bigger deal when some of the guys decided to give their rings to their girlfriend to wear on their finger or on a gold chain around their neck. Because the guy's fingers were normally much bigger than the girls, tape would be wrapped around the ring so that it would not slip off the digit. Not to be outdone, and to prove my true feeling about Carolyn Kay, the ring transfer took place. However, because of my small hands, no tape was necessary. She could barely get it over her knuckle. When our friends noted the smallness of the ring, it turned out not to be one of my most masculine days. However, there was more embarrassment on the horizon.

I noticed over a period of time that some of the couples had moved on to the next symbol of their affection. "Real rings" started showing up on the girl's fingers. These were not diamond or engagement-looking rings, but they were clearly bought to indicate something special. My first thought when I saw them was, *How much did that cost?* Worrying about cost doesn't sound very romantic, but I had limited resources—as in no resources

For a while I was able to avoid the obvious question of when I was going to buy Carolyn Kay a ring. However, the peer pressure was closing in. Rarely did a day go by that one of Carolyn's friends didn't suggest that I needed to get my act together because she was getting restless. I'm not sure if this was the friend's idea or if she was the messenger, but I was in a panic. Carolyn Kay was my life, so off I went to the jewelry store with my college money.

In retrospect, it would have been better if I had continued to avoid the purchase. In a small town with only one jewelry store and everyone knowing everyone else's business, just entering the premises caused stress. This was especially true when I knew that I couldn't afford to be there, but I was too afraid to leave.

In the end I bought the cheapest ring that I could find, and it looked cheap. I recall that it cost me around eighteen dollars. Instead of being proud of what I was about to do, I started counting up in my head how many hours I needed to work at seventy-five cents an hour to replenish my higher education fund.

Carolyn Kay never indicated any disappointment, but the feedback from her friends was less than rewarding—peer pressure can be cruel. Even today that episode remains an embarrassing memory of my youth. I know that I handled it in the only way that was financially possible at the time, but the lesson that I learned would never leave me. This was one of several happenings in my youth that drove my desire for a higher education, a good job, and a stable financial life. I did not want to be poor any longer.

I thought Carolyn Kay understood because our relationship continued to flower. My memories are that we were together all the time. We didn't have many classes together, but that was probably for the best. We did share a Spanish class, and I remember that she was much more proficient than I was. I had enough trouble with the King's English, so conjugating Spanish verbs was way beyond the possible. However, she never teased me about it.

Things were great. I started thinking of the way ahead, the future. We would go to college, get married, have a family, and become a power couple. We would grow old, knowing that we had been together our entire lives. At age seventeen, these were huge thoughts. And then one day the relationship was over.

I had started getting these signals from her girlfriends that Carolyn was interested in dating others. By now I had learned that the way you find out things about your relationship is from someone other than your partner, so I knew this was serious. I don't remember that Carolyn and I had any particular quarrels or disagreements, but it was clear that things were cooling. I also don't remember a time when she said "We are finished" or anything like that. The dating just seemed to stop.

My first big heartbreak was more than difficult. I had not only lost my friend, and girlfriend, I had lost my position of importance that being with her had afforded. But thanks to her, with my newfound confidence, I was ready to face the world with a new vision of my capabilities

Shortly after "the end," I became aware that she had already moved on and there was a new special guy in her life. Till this day, I don't know exactly why the relationship ended, but it did. Perhaps it was just time. Perhaps it was because he was better looking than me, perhaps because he was a better jock, or maybe it was that damn ring!

The remainder of my high school days seem like a blur from a social standpoint. I never again had a serious girlfriend, and even the senior prom seemed unimportant. I didn't get a prom date until about three days before the event, but it turned out just fine. In the wake of my disappointment, I got a little more serious about my grades and started to think about what I really wanted to study in college. Perhaps that is the silver lining to my disappointment.

As usual, all things happen for a reason, and there are lessons to be learned. Carolyn Kay went her way, and I went mine. We both had wonderful families, and we both had success in our professional endeavors. However, best of all—today I still count Carolyn Kay as one of my very best friends. We talk periodically on the telephone, and when we do, it is special. Maybe it's just me, but I think there is still a spark.

*The crown that I wore the night that Carolyn Kay and I were chosen the "ideal couple" at Fairbury High School's all-school mixer. Extremely worn and deteriorating but such a fond memory.*

## CHAPTER 18

## Charlie

————

When you are in your high school years, you never know what each of your classmates will end up doing with their life. The tendency is to believe that the captain of the football team, or even the best-looking girl, will be famous and rich. But reality is different. There are times that the valedictorian goes on to be president of a large and successful business, and then there are times that the valedictorian becomes something much less than everyone expected. I invite readers to recall their graduating class, and you will see what I mean. Additionally, I would advise young high school folks to look around at their classmates and just wonder what they think will become of each. Twenty to thirty years from now you will be very surprised.

All high school classes have students whom everyone knows and likes, but he or she is really not included in various social activities. The reasons vary, but most of the time nobody can give you a good reason—they just aren't included. As a result, you just never get to know some students. You never find out what they are made of, how they really react to situations, what they believe in, and what they think about the world.

Charlie was one of the most likable people in our class. He was a fun-loving student, always sporting a smile, and was always first in line when there was a prank to be played. He never really got in trouble, in school or out, but it seemed like he was just one step ahead of the administration all the time. Maybe that is why he was so liked

There was an iconic song that was popular at the time with lyrics that said, "Charlie Brown, you're a clown," and the fact that Charlie's last name was Brown seemed to enhance his position as the court jester. Publically, Charlie seemed to like his comparison with the lyrical character, but I sensed that privately he did not appreciate it. I think the song forced him further into a niche that was not the real

Charlie. As time would tell, Charlie was much more than a class prankster

After graduation, most of us lost touch with Charlie. However, because of my career in the military I was able to periodically track his whereabouts. Charlie had joined the Navy after graduation, and his specialty was as a medical corpsman.

First of all, the reader needs to understand that not just everyone can be selected for this rating in the Navy. It takes a special personality and calling, but apparently Charlie was very good at it. Not only did he successfully complete the initial training, he was later selected to serve as an independent corpsman. Independent corpsmen are those few that are assigned to direct combat units. By direct combat units, I mean ships at sea or Marine units in eye-to-eye contact with the enemy. These corpsmen are alone in the field with their shipmates or Marines, with no supervision of a doctor or other medical staff. Independent corpsmen are a special breed, and they are involved in a job where they are the substitute for a doctor, sometimes in isolated, lonely, and dangerous areas. They have a special ability and personality that allows them to administer medical assistance to shipmates who have been wounded in battle and may otherwise not make it home. Not everyone has the skill and compassion to work on a patient when you know that a buddy may die in their arms. I have served with Navy corpsmen in isolated areas, and I can tell you that the troops trust these guys with their lives.

These were the Vietnam years, and Charlie was assigned to a Marine Corps unit operating in country. This is not the place to discuss actual episodes, but let's just say that Charlie got a lot of "on-the-job training." His Marines loved him because he was very good at his job. To this day, he doesn't talk much about those harrowing days, but when he does, it is not about specific events. To Charlie, it was about the camaraderie and love that existed between those that faced danger together. His brotherhood.

Charlie came back into my personal life at the fifteenth high school reunion. By this time Charlie was out of the service and back in Fairbury, employed as a door-to-door mailman. As a Navy Lieutenant Commander at that time, I was in the initial stages of my career. Even though Charlie and I never directly discussed it, we knew that because of our mutual military background, we had a common bond. Besides, he never knew that I had been watching his progress while he was in the Navy. You could just feel his love and respect when we talked. I hope that he understood how I felt about him. During the reunion, there was the meeting hug between Charlie and me, and then we each moved on to greet other classmates. Later in the evening, Charlie asked if I would go with him out to his car. I didn't know what was going to happen or what to expect, but I said yes. What happened next really put a lump in my throat.

Charlie dug around in his car for a few minutes and came up with a ball cap. The ball cap was orange in color and had a silhouette of an elephant on the front. I had no idea what organization or company this ball cap was supposed to represent, and to this very day, still do not. My guess is that the cap was from a seed company or some other local agrarian enterprise, but I'm not sure. I asked Charlie, but either he didn't know or didn't want to say. However, he was insistent that I take the cap. He just kept saying that he wanted me to have it as a token of our friendship. This almost brought me to tears because Charlie and I had never been close in school. But then I realized that it was our chosen careers that he was talking about. The ball cap was a simple gift, but the meaning was not. Little did I know then how important that ball cap would be during the remainder of my career.

For years I wore that cap at every duty station and in many countries around the world. I nearly wore it out. The band in back of the cap had to be replaced because it just rotted away. It became so dirty that it ended up in the laundry, and almost did not survive the spin cycle. My children all knew how special that cap was to me, and they would tease me about what a relic it had become. But knowing how special the cap was to me, one of my daughters even asked if she could have it when I was gone. I knew that if he had known about this special request, Charlie would have been happy too.

It was not until the thirtieth high school reunion that I again saw Charlie face-to-face. Over the previous fifteen years we had only seen each other when I was home on leave, and then only momentarily. But that cap had always kept Charlie in my thoughts. I knew he had been a war hero, and the cap was my reminder to never forget.

As the evening of our thirtieth social event wore on, Charlie appeared by my side and asked if I would again go with him to his car. The answer was obvious.

This time it was clear that he had been planning the evening because there was no rummaging around in the car. In short order Charlie produced another ball cap. This one was blue with Marine Corps markings and labeled with the name of the unit that Charlie had served with in 'Nam. He told me that he had just been to a reunion with his old buddies, and he wanted me to have the cap. I tried to explain to him that I could not take it because this cap was clearly very special to him. I should have saved my breath because when we left his car, I was in custody of another treasured gift.

Over the years I continued to wear the elephant cap, but I didn't wear the Marine Corps hat much. I just didn't want to soil it or risk losing it. The USMC cap remained on my desk everywhere I went, so that I could see it and remember its significance

I was very lucky in my career, and as a result, I continued to be promoted. As my career flourished, I decided to start a tradition with Charlie's USMC cap. When I was promoted and awarded new collar devices, I would also attach one to Charlie's cap. So, through the years the cap was adorned with a Navy Captain's eagle, then replaced with a Rear Admiral lower half star, then the two stars of a Rear Admiral, and finally the three stars of a Vice Admiral. It made me very proud each time the cap received new apparel

I knew what I wanted to eventually do with that cap, and I got my opportunity at the fiftieth class reunion. It was my turn to give Charlie a cap. In front of our classmates, I told the story of Charlie's caps and how I had cherished their presence. I told Charlie how I had promoted his cap each time that I was promoted, and a proper ceremony had been held. I then presented him with his USMC cap, but it had been altered since he last saw it. Just above the USMC emblem were three shiny silver stars. I think he was happy.

That was the last time that I saw Charlie, but I think of him often, especially when I wear the elephant cap. In my mind I still see Charlie as a skinny kid who was a school trickster. But what he did in a time of war for his fellow warriors also sticks with me. How could we have known fifty years ago that someday Charlie would be a hero? To my knowledge, he is the only hero in our class. It bothers me that not more people know about his accomplishments, but one thing is for sure—Charlie will never tell them. He is a true hero.

## CHAPTER 19

## The Water Tower

———————

Even though I'm a believer, I was not what you would call a dyed-in-the-wool religious person. That being said, church and the happenings in the religious community were a big part of my young life. Early every Sunday morning I would find myself in Sunday school, and after that, I would reluctantly attend the regular church service. I say reluctantly because I had trouble sitting still and not talking to my friends for the hour of pulpit pounding. In Sunday school I could get away with my childish ways, but not so much with a full congregation of adults. Sunday evenings was when our church youth group met, so it was back to the church for another session. In addition to these weekly gatherings, there always were various church trips, festivities, exhibits, and conferences that needed to be attended.

Mom and Dad did not really push me in the direction of church attendance, but they didn't need to. The real reason I liked to attend was because that was where all my friends were, and to me, every gathering was primarily a social event. I hope the good Lord won't punish me for that because I did learn a great deal about the Bible.

As in most adventures, youthful planning starts off as a nonserious discussion with a lot of laughter. People start throwing out ideas about pranks that need to be accomplished but are so outrageous that everybody knows that they can't be done. Or perhaps so stupid that they shouldn't be tried in the first place. And then there is more laughter! That is how it all started one Sunday evening in the church basement after a youth session, during my senior year of high school.

What made the ensuing event so much more improbable was the cast of characters that would play the major roles. Maybe in those days I could have been portrayed as a youngster with a dark future, but the rest of this particular band of idiots were usually quiet, "follow-the-rules" kinds of kids. I'll take the blame because I think it was my idea to paint the water tower.

First of all, it is important to distinguish who was not part of the escapade, and that was my best friend Bob. After close consultation, we realized that if we got caught during this Davinci party, the county judge might come into play. As the judge's son, Bob's presence in the dock before the court would not look good in the local newspaper. I am not proud of the fact that I tried to convince the crew that Bob being with us might save us, but I was outvoted, and in the end Bob was not invited.

We were all seniors except Lynn, who was a year behind us in school. However, it was determined that his presence was necessary because of his athletic prowess. That was a stupid reason for including Lynn because there was nothing athletic about the caper, but we all liked Lynn.

Jim was probably the most accomplished prankster in the group and, therefore, an essential conspirator in the planning. Additionally, he was the tallest of the group, and that would turn out to be extremely important to the success of the mission.

I think Dick got included as an innocent bystander just because he was at a church meeting when a felony was being planned. Don't get me wrong. Dick was a willing participant, but as one of the very nice kids in town, this was not something that he would normally be a part of.

The minister's son, Gary, was not immune to fun-loving acts of youth, so adding him to the cast was an easy decision. The remaining important piece of the gang was to recruit a driver who was good at the wheel and could be relied on not to bolt under pressure if we had to go to plan B (there wasn't a plan B).

Gene would get the call to be the driver, and it was an easy decision. You see, Gene had been crippled his entire life and could not walk without crutches. This did not prevent him from living life normally and that included driving a nice new car. His car was uniquely rigged so that everything was accomplished by hand from the steering wheel location, and he was one heck of a good driver. We needed Gene not only for driving but also because he did not mind the thought of danger. In fact, it was as if he thought it might be fun to get caught. That scared me a little, but not enough to abort the mission.

All in all, this was an unlikely concoction of humanity, banded together to commit a high-order prank that was only one hour old in planning. We were all friends, but not guys who ran together most of the time. Except for attendance at church events, all six of us had never hung out together, but that night our hearts beat as one as we faced the giant steel behemoth—the water tower.

I do not recall where the paint and brushes came from, but the color was red and appropriate because that was one of the school colors. The church parking lot was the gathering scene where we went over last-minute planning. Gene determined that the car needed to be slightly altered to improve the clandestine nature of our mission. As such, using tape we borrowed from the church tool closet, we taped shut the car door light switches. That way, when the car doors were opened, the car dome lights would not come on and give away our location. The theft of that tape started us down the road that could have landed us in jail.

Every town in the Midwest, that I know of, has a water tower that supplies the pressure necessary for the operation of the town potable water supply. Just as it was in Fairbury, the towers are normally located on the highest ground in or around the town. In addition to the height of the tower, the high ground increases the hydraulic pressure in the system and ensures the citizens a strong flow of water during their morning showers. Fairbury's tower was at the north end of town, in a relatively low population area, which was not hard to find in a town of only three thousand souls. Actually, the tower was only a few blocks from my house, but that was not unusual; everything in town was only a few blocks from my house. Still, we needed to be cautious because a cruising carload of kids in a remote part of town could be seen as suspicious. Additionally, the single police car that the town owned was deemed a threat.

It was about ten thirty p.m. when Gene circled the area of the tower several times to make sure there was no one on the street. Folks in Fairbury went to bed early, so we didn't anticipate interruption, but you couldn't be too safe. As we approached the drop zone at the foot of the tower, Gene slowed to just a couple of miles per hour. We crouched on the floorboard of the car and then opened the car doors. The taped switches worked perfectly because the car dome lights did not come on. One by one, armed with paint and brushes, we rolled out of the slowly moving car into the grassy ditch. We laid still for a few moments to get our bearings, while Gene slowly cruised away. After a couple of deep breaths, we looked up at the sixty-five feet of steel girder legs and tank that awaited our assault.

I was probably the most adventurous of this group, but I remember thinking, *What the hell am I doing?* If we got caught, my dad would have killed me before the authorities had a chance to exact legal punishment. I put the thought in the back of my mind, and we moved to the base of the structure. One leg of the tower had a ladder attached that ended forty feet up, at the base of the tank. Then there was a very narrow walkway, or catwalk, that went around the entire circumference of the tank.

It was decided that there was not enough room for all of us on the tank, so after a short discussion, Jim was selected to make the ascent to the catwalk. We figured that Jim was taller and, therefore, had a longer arm span and would be able to paint larger letters. We wanted to make sure that this was a professional and envied job. We were sure that other classmates were going to be jealous that they had not been included. After Jim's selection to make the initial ascent, I sensed a sigh of relief from a couple of the troops. Jim commenced the climb to the top, and I went up the ladder behind him. I stopped just under the catwalk so I could assist in handling the paint and brushes. When I got into position, I realized what a good decision we had made about only one person going onto the catwalk. That thing was only eighteen inches wide, and to me it looked smaller than that. One of Jim's shoes filled up the entire width of the walk, and he had to hug the tank every time he moved. His movements were more of a shuffle than a walk. Two of the other guys also climbed partway up the ladder to form a human chain of war-fighting supplies. It seemed to take forever, but I know that Jim was working fast because I could hear the swoosh of the brush and the shuffle of his feet as he worked his way around the tank.

I did not have to say "Move" twice when the painting was complete. Everyone scampered down that ladder and assembled in the ditch, alongside the adjacent road. Gene's timing was superb, and as he slowed to almost a stop, we rapidly entered the car. There was a lot of excitement, with teenage laughter about how we had pulled off the coup of the year without getting caught. Gene drove back to the church to put some distance between the crime scene and the perpetrators. We really wanted to find a location that we could see our handiwork—the anticipation was killing us—but it was so dark that night that you could not see anything. We would have to wait until morning

As I prepared for school the next day, I tried to look inconspicuous to my folks as I looked out the back window of our house, toward the water tower only two blocks away. I looked and then looked again. Then I squinted and looked again. You could see that something had been painted on the tower, but it was almost too small to read "Class of 59." It was so small that I doubt that the authorities even knew that a crime had been committed. Disappointment reigned supreme.

During that school week, the six of us quietly discussed the disappointment. We decided that we would have to make another assault after our youth meeting the following Wednesday. This problem had to be fixed. Classmates were talking about the paint job, but it was clear that they thought it was a puny effort. I felt fortunate that they didn't know who was involved because that could have ruined my reputation for the entirety of my senior year. *If you are going to do something, do it right* is what my dad used to say.

Everyone assumed their appointed positions on the following Wednesday, and away we went for another assault. Actually, the second time of breaking the law seemed to be much easier. Just like the original approach, everything went smoothly, and we were at the base of the tower in no time. This time we were armed with silver paint to erase the original letters and red paint to institute a larger-sized message. As before, Jim scaled the ladder to the top and commenced the silver paint-out. He seemed to be a lot more comfortable on the ledge this time because the erasing job went swiftly.

Now it was time to get this job completed properly, and we had done some good preplanning. We realized that we needed a bigger arm span, but Jim was the biggest guy we had, so we needed an arm extension. Looking back, we didn't plan as well as we could have because a brush on a stick would have been a superior idea. However, we didn't do that—wish we had. What we did next scared the hell out of me, but I couldn't show fear.

Jim took his position on the narrow catwalk, and I climbed on his shoulders. Yes, I know this is stupid.

There I was, forty feet above the ground, standing on Jim's shoulders with no railings, on eighteen inches of corrugated steel, with a paintbrush and can of paint in my hands—petrified. Jim would shuffle, and I would make large sweeping letters of red. Then Jim would take the brush and complete the letters on the bottom end, while I concentrated on maintaining my balance on his shoulders. No doubt about it, we should have taken a broomstick and a role of tape.

The next day when I looked out of my mom's kitchen window, it was obvious that this time there would be no question that the tower was properly painted. It was poor handwriting, and you could see where my penmanship and Jim's didn't quite match up, but "CLASS OF 59" was prominent. Kind of made me proud.

A week later, it happened to be one of our periodic family get-togethers, and it was being held at the Optimist Club clubhouse, which was located within a half block of the water tower. I recall standing next to my dad and my uncle as they looked up and discussed what should be done to the delinquents that painted the tower. My dad could be pretty salty at times, and he called the culprits some very nasty names. I cringed when I heard him say what he would do if he caught the teenage miscreants.

Many years later I thought about telling him that I was one of those class of '59 banditos. After all, to my knowledge, all six of us had turned out just fine, and we had become well-behaved citizens in our advanced years. Besides, the statute of limitations must have run out by then. In the end I decided to let that portion of my life remain an untold story. You never can tell, even in Dad's old age, he might have whipped up on me. But I like to believe that he would have laughed.

There are some things that parents should not know about their children until much, much later in life. Most of those secrets are only preserved through the art of not getting caught.

## CHAPTER 20

## Hangouts

---

The total existence of my childhood can be measured by counting the amount of time that I spent in a finite number of hangouts or activities. Because there was no internet or TV or cell phones, I tended to do things that would allow me to be out of the house, face-to-face with my friends as much as possible. There weren't a lot of places to go, so I would normally end up in the same places over and over again. I always get a giggle from my kids and younger friends when I try to explain what we did to have fun in the 1950s. At the same time, I feel sorry for them because of the social interaction that they have missed. Times change, but I'm sure glad that I had my time when I did.

## The Square

There was no activity more prevalent in my life than just driving my car around the square, over and over again, hoping that I'd see one of my friends doing the same thing. The square, of course, was the center of town. Just like every other small Nebraska town, the courthouse stood in the middle of this four-block adventure—The Square. There were no stop signs or stoplights to cause you to slow down as you made the two-minute trip around the square. Only the occasional appearance of the town's single police car would cause you to decelerate. However, you never went very fast anyway. That would have defeated the purpose of cruising around the square.

What I'm about to say now doesn't have anything to do with my nightly travels around the square, but Fairbury's courthouse was interesting and had quite a history. It was always entertaining to hang out next to the lower-level jail windows and have a discussion with whomever was incarcerated. In all of those discussions, I never met one guy who was not innocent, at least in his own mind.

History buffs could find bullet holes in the courthouse that had existed since the Ma Barker gang put them there in the 1930s while robbing the First National Bank, which stood on the northeast corner of the square. All but one of the gang got away with the loot. One was found dead a few miles out of town. The story goes that Herb, a young man on a motorcycle, slid his bike to a stop next to a downed policeman, grabbed the policeman's machinegun, and filled the getaway car with holes, dealing one of the bad guys a mortal wound. My dad loved telling that story because Dad and everyone else in town knew the hero.

The only time you couldn't circle the square without interruption was on certain summer Saturday evenings when the north side was shut down for the square dance. I was not much of a square dancer, so I just altered my travels to three sides of the square.

No matter how early I started my circular trek around the square, everything else that I did in an evening started on the square and was determined by who I met there. Even fifty years later, when I visit Fairbury, I drive around the square, but usually only once. I don't want to look like an old weird guy.

And besides, there are now two stoplights.

## Scouting

Cub Scouts and Boy Scouts are organizations that I have fond memories of, even though I wasn't very accomplished at earning merit badges and getting promoted. My friend Bob and several others were aggressive in their pursuit of excellence, while I thought of the scouting activities as a time to just be with the guys. Actually, I was pretty good at all the necessary scout achievements. I was really good at fire building, bird identification, cooking, camping, and citizenship, but I lacked the desire to go get it documented and signed off in my logbook. I knew that I could do all the stuff, but getting it signed off just didn't seem to be important. Oh, I was a "Life Scout" and a member of the "Order of the Arrow," but "Eagle Scout" was a bridge too far.

The scouting activities were what was important to me. I loved the camping and the jamborees; the various events and just getting together for the meetings were something I looked forward to. Memorial Day, which used to be called Decoration Day, was always a hot and sweaty time of year, but I enjoyed getting into my uniform because the scouts directed traffic at the cemetery. I know it's hard for the reader to understand, but in those days everybody, and I mean everybody, showed up at the cemetery to lay flowers at the gravesites. It made me feel very proud and important to be involved.

One of my favorite scouting activities was during the football season because our troop would travel the seventy miles to Lincoln, where we got to be ushers at the Cornhusker game. Now, that was special.

The annual scout kite flying contest was held at the airport, and there were prizes for everything from biggest and smallest kites to the prettiest kite, to the most well-constructed kite, and of course, to the most unique. However, the prize that I pursued was for the highest flyer. After several years of getting whipped by superior competition, I had learned that the most important part of a successful high-flying kite system was an adequate amount of very strong string or line. There was an enormous amount of drag on the line when the kite was high, especially in a heavy wind. I had lost too many kites to insufficient line strength, and I had determined that that was not going to happen again. As a result, I spent an entire year collecting line from everywhere that I could find it and then carefully knotting it together with a scout bowline. One of the strongest lines that I discovered was fishing line because it was not only strong, it was light. Dad and Grandpa stepped in when it was clear that I needed a dispenser for all the line because there was no way I was going to be able to control the pull of a large kite with my bare hands. They constructed a large spindle in a cradle with a hand crank that I could use to reel in and let out the line as necessary. Then they built a seat on top of the spindle so I could sit on it as I controlled the kite. Without the spindle and seat, the high winds on the kite would have just dragged my diminutive body along the ground.

On the day of the contest there were moderate winds, but a lot of kids were experiencing the loss of kites because of the same problem that I had experienced in previous years. Mine however, was flying high and steady.

The winner of the contest needed to be determined by accurate measurement, so a Piper Cub airplane took off to go up and measure the altitude of the competitors. I knew I had finally cracked the winner's circle when the aircraft dipped his wings several times over the top of my entrant. After a long year of preparation, it was a great day for Dad, Grandpa, and me. We celebrated with homemade ice cream.

In another event, all of the Cub Scouts would gather on an annual basis for a competition that got my and Dad's competitive juices flowing. The city fathers would seal off a five-block downhill course on one of the steepest town streets where a competition of soapbox derby racing could take place. At the top of the hill, an elevated starting gate was erected so the race cars could get a fast start as they began the downhill cruise.

None of the kids my age were capable of building a competitive vehicle by themselves, so the parents were involved in the construction. As far as my dad was concerned, this was one of those "just win, baby" events. I'm pretty sure that when I won, which I often did, he saw it as his win over the other parents. During the year, Dad was always trying to find wheels that had better ball bearings and a steering mechanism that gave me more control. My guess is that he even indulged in some intelligence gathering on the other parents, just to see what the competition was going to show up with. Once in a while he'd come home all excited about how to make the car faster.

On the day of the race, after Dad had verified that the wheels were properly greased and all the car systems were in proper working order, I would get detailed driving instructions on how to keep my head down so there was efficient air flow over the hood.

Parents today would go nuts seeing these brakeless wooden crates screaming downhill, little kids at the wheel without helmets or other protective devices. We didn't know any better, and anyway, nobody ever got hurt. After every qualifying event, Dad would critique my driving, which never was perfect, But thank goodness, it was good enough. The entire town would be there cheering, but I could hear my dad, yelling at the top of his lungs to "steer straight, steer straight" as I plunged down the hill. Dad always seemed hyped about anything involving a prize, and it was to my benefit not to let him down. They didn't give out a merit badge for soapbox racing, but thanks to Dad I was the best there was in Fairbury.

All in all, I spent so much time with the scouts, and I learned so many things in the scouting system, that those times deserve a treasured place on my list of hangouts.

**Fishing**

Fishing was another one of those activities that just seemed natural to me. As a result, I spent many hours watching a bobber at Crystal Springs and setting lines on a muddy Little Blue River bank. From the time that I was old enough to ride a bike, I would take my fishing pole and ride across town and then three miles into the countryside in order to fish for bullheads. I'm not sure if the town or the county owned Crystal Springs, but the four lakes—really ponds—were a great place for a young man to enjoy a warm summer day. Mom and Dad did not seem to be concerned about my lonesome adventures into the countryside. In fact, there was some encouragement for me to go when there was an urge for a fish dinner

Bullheads were more easily caught using worms as bait, so Dad and I always had a can of night crawlers that we kept in a cool corner of the basement. Bullheads are a member of the catfish family, I think, but they are a lot smaller than their river relatives. If I caught a bullhead that weighed a pound, I had a big fish. Most of them came in at a half pound or less. That meant that I needed to catch a mess of fish if we were to have a meal. That also meant that someone had to clean all those fish, and that was a job I didn't like, but I did it.

Once in a while I would fish for carp, which were a lot bigger and more fun to catch, but they were very hard to prepare and eat because they had scales and were full of bones.

Mom liked to eat fish, but she complained about their fishy smell, a complaint that seemed strange to me. As a result, she had a preparation trick that removed some of the wild-gamey taste of the catch. Once the fish were cleaned, she would put them in a tray and cover the fish in salt water, where they would stay in the refrigerator overnight. The trick seemed to work because the next day the fish cooked up into the delicious white flaky meal that Dad and I were fond of, and Mom didn't complain about the odor

River fishing was something that I tried to do as often as possible when I got a little older because river catfish were a lot bigger and more fun to catch than the bullheads that I was used to. Dad and I did some river fishing when I was young, but it wasn't until I got my driver's license that I could really spend a lot of effort in catching the big fish. Transportation was necessary because I needed to carry a lot of poles and get to an area well north of town on the Little Blue River. I always fished upstream, north of town, because I had seen the sewage that flowed into the river near the town power plant dam. There was no way I was eating a fish that had been feeding on what came out of that sewer pipe.

River fishing is usually done at night and requires many poles if you hope to be successful. The poles weren't fancy, just branches off of nearby trees, but they could be used over and over again, as long as they had some flexibility. The pole was just pushed deep into the muddy river bank or wedged into a pile of logs and branches that had damned up under a bridge or along the river's edge. The line was never long, and sometimes I would actually hang the bait just an inch or two above the surface of the water. Big catfish spend most of their time on the bottom, feeding and sleeping, but at night they will come right out of the water to gobble a tasty frog dangling from a hook. You couldn't river fish every night because it would just wear you out. Once the lines were set, you needed to run, or check the lines, every couple of hours during the night. My brother Randy was six years younger than me, but he also loved to fish, so the folks would let me take him along during some of my nightly runs. Wandering around on a slippery river bank in the dark while inspecting twenty-five or thirty lines could take you awhile, and there were hazards involved. However, the excitement of the catch was worth it, and Randy wanted to be part of the fun

One moonlit night, about midnight, Randy and I parked the car near a bridge that had a nearby path leading down to the water's edge. We had planted a number of poles in the area earlier in the evening, and it was time to see if we were eating fish in the morning. As we walked across the bridge in the silent darkness, we both heard a noise that sounded like the thrashing of bushes, and it sounded like it was coming from under the bridge. Peering over the edge of the bridge, in the moonlight, we could identify the source of the commotion. The large log jam that was piled up under the bridge was jumping up and down. Excitement set in because we both knew that one of our poles had been planted in that very place. We made our way across the bridge and down the path and then carefully out onto the moving woodpile. We found our pole with a very tight line, which we both grabbed and tried to pull. Our footing was not very good, and it was clear that we were not making any progress. Another tactic was going to be necessary if we were going to retrieve the beast at the other end of the line.

I didn't let on, but I was scared about the plan that I was about to share with Randy. But something had to be done. We couldn't let this prize winner get away. Randy's eyes got big as I stripped down to my underwear and told him to hang onto the pole because I was going into the river and push up on whatever was down there, while he pulled. I grabbed hold of the woodpile so I wouldn't get swept down the river and then disappeared beneath the surface. I had not realized that the water depth there was about six to seven feet, which was unusual for the shallow Little Blue River. I cautiously worked my way down the taut line until I came to an abrupt stop. My hands spread out across the face of the biggest catfish I had ever seen, and I hadn't even seen him yet. I shot out of the water to explain to Randy, who now had even bigger eyes, what we were faced with. Brother just nodded when I explained to him that I was going back down, and he was to pull like hell.

Luckily, I was still wearing tennis shoes because after I got both my hands into the fish's gills, I was able to stand on the rough bottom of the river while I pushed up as hard as I could. Fortunately, by this time the fish was about worn out. Between the pulling and the pushing, the monster was hoisted onto the wood dam.

It was early morning by the time we got home, but we received a hero's welcome from Dad, while Mom voiced concern about our tardiness and the safety of little Randy. Turned out that thirty-two pounds was not near the Jefferson County record, but it was the biggest that I had ever caught.

## The Mill

Up until the time I was about fourteen, I spent a lot of time at the Planning Mill, the local lumberyard, because that is where my grandfather worked. Grandpa Jones was a very accomplished cabinetmaker, and I loved watching him do his magic with a few boards, nails, screws, and glue.

Almost all of the tools at the mill were operated by hand, with very few automated devices. There was some big equipment, but as far as I was concerned, the huge rotating saws were too noisy and not very safe. I was probably biased because it was not uncommon to get a phone call from Grandma announcing that Grandpa had lopped off another finger and he was on his way to the hospital. In fact, I don't remember Grandpa having a full finger on either hand, but that didn't seem to detract from his ability to turn out a beautiful product.

I was always impressed to see how much manpower and manual labor went into a simple piece of furniture. The wood was cut with a handsaw, on a straighter line than most people could imagine, and holes for screws were drilled with a hand drill that required significant patience while turning a crank. When the lumber needed to be fitted or sized, it was done with a hand plane that reduced the thickness of the wood. You needed a steady hand to get a uniform board width, one board shaving at a time. No power tools for my grandpa.

The big rotating blade of one saw was four feet in diameter and was only used when you needed a rough cut of a large piece of wood. The saw was operated by a belt that was about ten feet long and connected to the only electric motor in the mill. When powered up, the belt would flap, the motor would whine, and the blade would screech until it was finally up to speed. The noise coming out of that saw was scary to me. Whenever it was operating, I would make myself scarce. I was too young to lose some fingers.

When Grandpa had completed a work of art, it was time to deliver it to a lucky customer, using the Planning Mill truck. These deliveries were fun trips for me because the truck had no doors and I could hang out of the vehicle as we passed through the town. The truck was old, but it was also missing a lot of parts because it had been modified to carry whatever needed to be carried. I don't remember what model or year it was, but in addition to no doors, there was no hood over the motor, and the bed of the truck was just a flat platform with no sides. The door removal made sense because the driver and the passenger could hold onto long pieces of lumber while still sitting in the cab. Delivery of finished furniture was the part of Grandpa's job that I enjoyed the most.

In addition to all the pieces of wood that I needed for the construction of clubhouses and tree houses, the Planning Mill was a valuable source of sawdust. I fancied myself a good athlete, and as I approached high school age, I needed to practice my athletic skills at high jumping. I wanted to be ready to compete. As such, I built my own high-jumping bar in the vacant lot across the alley from our house, but

I needed a lot of sawdust in the pit to soften my landings. Luckily, there was an endless supply of sawdust at the mill. No one seemed to care when Dad and Grandpa brought bags of the stuff home each night after work. I guess you could say that Grandpa and the old mill were a very strong link in my chain of growing-up experiences.

**The Bottling Company**

The Coca-Cola bottling company was another one of my favorite haunts during my early youth because that is where Dad worked, and I was treated like a company mascot. There were only five or six employees, in addition to my dad, but I knew everyone and everyone knew me. When I was in the plant, I was allowed run around, climb on the empty soda cases, and sit in the trucks, anytime I wanted. I always enjoyed my days in the plant. Even in the 1940s the bottling company was a pretty automated place, and I was intrigued with all the moving parts required to mix the Coke, wash the bottles, and then fill each bottle to the proper level.

The bottling plant seemed really large to me then, but actually it was just a medium-sized open warehouse that was adequate for producing the soda and also housing the three trucks that the company

306

owned. The actual bottling of the beverage took place in the front of the building, where there was a large window, so that passersby could stop and watch the evolution. However, I got to be in the building, right there to witness the action, up close and personal.

In addition to Coca-Cola, the plant also produced several other flavors, like Cream Soda and Orange Soda. So, during the week, the daily bottling was dedicated to the flavor of the day. When I entered the plant, I could take a deep breath and know right away what was being mixed for that day's bottling.

The soda was mixed in a large vat that sat on a second-floor mezzanine area, above the conveyer system that delivered the bottles. The liquid flowed through plastic tubing, and as each bottle passed the fill location, a mechanism would slam down on four bottles at a time while the fluid rapidly filled the bottles. About a foot down the conveyer line, another mechanical arm would reach down and cap the bottles as they proceeded to the inspection station. Mutt, the guy at the inspection station, had to be extremely quick and precise. In my opinion, he needed to be highly trained because things happened in a hurry at the end of the line.

Mutt would grab eight bottles at a time, four in each hand, and place them on a bright light table while he visually determined if they had the proper amount of liquid and that the coloring was correct. When he found a bad one, which happened periodically, he had to make a rapid discard, while putting the other seven bottles in an awaiting case. He then grabbed the next eight bottles that were accumulating for inspection. Meanwhile, another worker hauled the full case away, and an empty case was prepared for filling. I learned early on that I shouldn't spend too much time around the inspection station because things got thrown around a lot and there was a great deal of cursing.

Dad helped in the bottling effort, but his real job was to drive a truck and deliver the various sodas all over the county. His normal routine was to deliver to all the in-town stores three days a week and then deliver to all the little towns in the county on the other two days. I loved riding in the cab of the truck, especially during the out-of-town trips, because just passing the countryside and seeing the fields was a special treat. Back in those days we didn't do much family travel, so getting outside the city limits of town was a big adventure for me. Every little town had its mom-and-pop grocery store that needed to be resupplied with soda, but the bars and saloons were my favorite. There was just something special about entering a drinking establishment through the back door, winding your way through beer kegs and boxes, and then entering the premises behind the bar. I'm not sure why this impressed me, perhaps an omen of my future, but the smell of stale beer and wet cardboard boxes was remarkable.

When we arrived at a customer destination, Dad would load up a hand dolly with cases of soda from the truck, while I sat at the bar and ate or drank whatever treat the owner saw fit to give me. It seemed like all the proprietors were happy to see me because they would scratch my fuzzy head, talk to me like a customer, and provide something special for me to munch on while Dad worked. By the time Dad and I had completed a daily supply run to all the outlying towns, my appetite for dinner was destroyed.

As I got older, I spent less and less time at the Coke plant, but I have fond memories of the long talks that Dad and I had, cruising along the dirt roads of Nebraska, en route to deliver Coca-Cola. That dusty, dirty, and hot truck cab was clearly one of my first hangouts.

## Camping

Summertime, especially in my younger days, was a time for spending all day outside, playing baseball, fishing, swimming, and of course, camping. In addition to the many nights that I spent under the stars with my brother and other friends, there were two annual camps for which I was always able to scrape up the money to attend. Both of these weekly camps added greatly to my growing-up process. Although only one week in duration, those seven days were filled with meeting new friends, learning new things about myself, enjoying being away from parents, and then experiencing the excitement of going home.

The YMCA camp was held at Camp Jefferson, which was located a few miles south of Fairbury, in some of the few hills that exist in Jefferson County. The camp area itself was very Spartan and consisted of ten small cabins, each named after an Indian tribe. Each could house eight boys for the week. I always stayed in the cabin named after the Algonquian tribe, but with different boys every year. I claimed the upper bunk bed closest to the door so I could quickly jump down and beat everybody to the first morning event.

In addition to the cabins, there was a larger building that served as our mess hall and a place for meetings. I remember the food being pretty good, and I always appreciated a kid-friendly meal after a hard day of playing. However, I was not very fond of KP (kitchen police) duty. I'm sure I only had KP duty a few times during the week, but it seemed like an excessive number of times when I could have been out enjoying other activities. Cleaning tables, handling dirty trays, and washing dishes was not my idea of having fun.

My favorite building in the entire camp was the crafts and woodworking shop that was filled with electric saws and tools that I could use to make Mom and Dad a camp keepsake. There was also plenty of braiding material to make bracelets and pocket watch lanyards for Grandpas and Grandmas, who, I was sure, wanted some camp memorabilia.

There was also a lake, which in reality was only a small pond, but there were rowboats that you could use at any time. My favorite rowboat pastime was to see if I could sneak up on the many turtles that were sunning themselves on logs that were lying in the water. It was a successful camping week if I returned home with a pet turtle or two.

The camp had a small swimming pool, but I did not like spending much time there. In today's world the health department would have shut that place down. Even as a ten-year-old I knew that an opaque pool of slimy water could not be good for you.

After a number of years of attending YMCA camp, I became a seasoned veteran and part of a group of old-timers who liked to play tricks on the new-comers. It didn't take much to convince a first-time camper that there were things he needed to learn if he was ever to be one of the special guys. We would spin a yarn that one of the "must-dos" at camp was to catch a "snipe." The story was that a snipe was a very small bird that couldn't fly but could run like a deer, and only showed himself shortly after the sun went down. A number of the little feathered guys had been spotted over the years along the path that led down to the lake. The new kids were always eager to take the gunnysacks that we would issue them and head out to sit in the weeds for most of the dark night, just so they could be the first great hunter to return with a snipe.

I exalted at their pain and disappointment, which I had once experienced, when they returned very late in the evening, empty-handed and embarrassed at their own naïveté.

The camp director was a man named CC Bailey, and I remember him as a whirlwind of energy and a fount of knowledge. He seemed to be everywhere, making sure that we were busy and that the camp was being run properly. I think he was originally from Wisconsin because he was always singing the Wisconsin fight song, which didn't go down well with all of us young Cornhusker fans. He was like a Captain Kangaroo type of character on steroids. I never did know if CC had another real job or what he did when he wasn't running the camp; however, it wasn't important because he oversaw one of the more important weeks in my year.

CC's main man for getting things done and helping us in the woodworking shop was a tall, thin man named Les. Les was very quiet, but always present when you needed him. I marveled at his ability to accurately and precisely cut wood with the electric band saw. He had a remarkable resemblance, and the same many abilities, of Mr. Green Jeans. Les would be gone from the camp for a few hours now and then to look after his real day job. He was the superintendent of the city cemetery and there were periodic grave diggings that just couldn't wait.

My Captain Kangaroo and Mr. Green Jeans taught me a lot over the course of several years, and I can't help but think that my adult ability to get along with all sorts of folks was born at Camp Jefferson.

My other summer camping memories center on my involvement in the Boy Scouts and the lessons that I learned at Camp Augustine in Grand Island, Nebraska. This annual trek took place when I was in my early teens, so the activities and experiences were totally different from my younger Camp Jefferson days.

Boy Scout camp was all about gathering knowledge that would help in your quest for merit badges and becoming a better person. I have to admit that

my heart was not really into some of the requirements, and, therefore, I didn't obtain as many merit
badges as others. On the other hand, my friend Bob
was a zealot when it came to filling up his uniform
sash with evidence of his knowledge. Don't get me
wrong, there were times, even today, when I envied
him for his zeal, but I didn't have the patience required for some events.

Bird-watching was not my strong suit, but Bob
would sit quietly in the woods all day, all by himself,
waiting to be the first scout to spot a bobolink. Now,
I know that a bobolink is a cool North American
songbird, but sitting around all day to see one of
those little finch-like raptors so I could get a small
piece of cloth was not something that I was prepared
to do. I suspect that is why Bob eventually became
an Eagle Scout and I did not.

I did listen carefully during the classes on cooking because part of the lesson plan was on identify-
ing herbs, grass, weeds, tubers, and other wild flora
that could be cooked and eaten. By the time that
the cooking class was over, I could prepare a mighty
tasty dandelion salad and a hearty wild onion soup.
I figured that this knowledge might keep me alive
someday, and I received a merit badge to boot.

A dish that I called Indian Chicken is one that I
would prepare several times in the many years that

followed my scouting days. The methodology was to dig a shallow hole and then line it with sizable rocks. After the rocks were in place, you built a fire on top of the rocks until they were plenty hot. While the rocks were heating, you took a whole chicken and wrapped it in corn husks, or in later years aluminum foil, which worked even better. The fire was then pulled out of the hole, exposing the hot interior. The chicken was then placed on top of the rocks. Once that was complete, you covered the rocks and chicken with dirt and rebuilt the fire on top of the dirt. Up until this point, this was an easy evolution, but the hard part was trying to figure out just how long you let the fire burn before you dig up the chicken again. I have to admit that I achieved a mixed success rate every time Indian Chicken was attempted. I've gotten everything from raw to unidentifiable charcoaled poultry. But again, I got the merit badge.

My days at camp were normally filled with physical activities, like matching my skills with the other scouts on the archery range or even learning how to build fires without a match. I figured that having a fire-starting capability would come in handy with my newfound cooking expertise.

The camp councilors always tried to keep us busy when there were no actual training sessions in progress. Actually, some of my most fun camp times were

during these quickly organized nontraining periods. The councilors would organize feats of physical skill, like who could do the most push-ups and
who could run the fastest. This gave me an opportunity to test myself against kids from all over the
state. I never was the best at any one event, but I was
among the top contenders in most events. I was especially quick and fast at that age, and when I went
to the starting line barefooted, I was tough to beat.
This success did a lot for my self-esteem. For the first
time I realized that it didn't make any difference if I
were big or small in stature or if I were from a tiny or
large town: I could compete.

There was not a significant amount of hazing at
Boy Scout camp, but with boys ranging in age, the
younger folks had to get used to some different
learning processes. And not all that I learned had to
do with scouting. Trying to get into the cliques and
private little clubs that the other scouts created for
themselves was not something that was easily done.
Bob's older brother, John, who was two years older,
and several of his friends had established a club, and
they called themselves the "Pythons." Later I would
understand that this name had been chosen because
of an anatomical superiority that they thought they
possessed. I knew John pretty well, and after all, he
was my best friend's brother, so Bob and I made an

attempt to join the group. We were quickly rebuffed, and it was declared that we needed to start our own group, and it was to be named "Grub Worms," A name with a connotation that was equally understood.

Even though I was not as aggressive in my pursuit of merit badges as many of the other scouts, I always felt like I had learned as much as they did. I just didn't have the signatures to prove it. If I had it to do over again, I would change that. That being said, I think that my fellow scouts had respect for my abilities because during my last summer of scouting camp, I was selected as a member of The Order of the Arrow. The Order of the Arrow recognizes scouts who best exemplify the scout oath and law in their daily lives. This is the National Honor Society of scouting, and the selection was a great and unexpected honor because members are selected by their peers.

Part of the initiation ceremony was to spend twenty-four hours in silence, all alone, in the woods. I was given a sleeping bag, but no food. My job was to survive and return the next day for the rest of the induction ceremony. I was really glad that I had taken that cooking class because I ate a lot of dandelions that night.

As I got into my late teens, I didn't go on any more overnight or weeklong camping trips. I seemed to have too many other things that were more important. But I knew if I had to make it in the wilderness, I could.

**Movie Theaters**

In the days of no television, cell phones, computers, CD players, or even record players, movie theaters played a big role in my life. Fairbury was fortunate that it had a theater because many small towns throughout the Midwest were not so lucky. In some towns the older kids, the ones with a driver's license, would drive twenty or thirty miles just to take their girlfriends to see a movie.

The Bonham Theater was built in 1926 by Universal Pictures as a place to not only showcase their own movies but also those of the rest of the booming film industry. So that the theater had a reasonable chance of success, Universal required that some local folks have some skin in the game, That is where Luther Bonham came into the picture. Luther was a cashier at the First National Bank and had a reputation for helping folks properly invest their assets. He set out to organize and coordinate a small group of investors who would assist Universal in the funding of the project.

The Bonham Theater opened on the twenty-eighth of September, 1926, and it must have been something to see. History records that on opening day three performances were held and a total of three thousand people attended. I'm sure that Luther logged the project as a success because the entire population of the town was right at three thousand in 1926. The investors must have also been smiling all the way to the First National Bank. For years to come, the Bonham Theater was known as the "Showplace of Southeast Nebraska."

For me, the Bonham was a place that I could learn about places and things throughout the world that I had not yet experienced firsthand. Every Saturday you could find me in the center of the theater, halfway back in the hardwood folding seats, enjoying a Roy Rogers, Gene Autry, or Hopalong Cassidy double feature. These cinema Wild West heroes influenced the way that I played cowboys and Indians in the backyard later that day. But my real movie learning experience came from the news reels that preceded every feature.

There was news about things that, up until then, I didn't even know existed. The president would be giving a speech, or a volcano would be erupting, or a new giant skyscraper was being built in New York City—all examples of news that caused me to realize that I really was a small-town kid and had a lot to learn. The news reels always had a sports spot, and judging from what was covered, Duke University must have had a terrific football team in the 1940s because their games were always in the reel. Armed with my box of Milk Duds or extra-large Tootsie Roll, I relaxed and enjoyed my weekly ritual of double features, all the time hating that there were seven days until the next movie.

One Saturday in 1949 sticks vividly in my mind as a learning experience that I will never forget. At eight years of age I didn't understand many worldly things, but I knew that what I was seeing on that day was important. It must have been important because on that special 1949 day there was a huge crowd assembled for the showing of a movie called *The Sands of Iwo Jima*, starring John Wayne. The city fathers had placed a huge flatbed truck in front of the theater and installed a microphone and speakers so that everybody could hear the event proceedings. The main speaker, before the movie, was someone whom I knew very well. And, as my years passed, this person would become more and more important in my opportunities to become successful in life. His name was Bob Denney, and he was the father of one of my best friends. I used to see Mr. Denney almost every day when I was at Barry's house. I knew he was a lawyer and an important man in town, but I was about to learn something about him that was clearly more important to everyone in town. Bob had been a Marine Corps captain and had taken part in the bloody World War II fight on the Pacific island of Iwo Jima. Later in life, history lessons would help me understand just how terrible that battle must have been. But that day, seeing Barry's father stand in front of the microphone and explain some of the things that he had seen and done was a real eyepopper for me. Up until that point, it had not even crossed my mind that he had been in the military. However, from that day forward, I saw Bob Denney in a much more reverent light. He was more than just my friend's dad, he was a hero, and the whole town knew it.

The theater had a balcony, but I did not frequent the upper region of the Bonham except on a few occasions. I'm not sure why because the seating was the same as below and the viewing was excellent. The one thing that I recall that might have influenced my decision to sit downstairs was the noise that came from the movie projectors. Just above and behind the balcony seats was the opening into the projector room, and you could clearly hear the whir of the film as it passed from one reel to the other. Movies always came on multiple reels, so there was also that commotion in the projector room as the operator attempted to coordinate the ending of one reel with beginning of the next. I think that I just did not like to be interrupted or distracted while I was watching my favorite cowboy movie.

Financial frugality was always an issue in my life, and even at eight years of age, I understood that going to the movie was not something that my parents were going to fund. After all, the entry fee to the Bonham was twelve cents for a youth, and that was also the cost of a loaf of bread. The thought of missing my dream world on Saturday afternoon was not something that I wanted to face, so I would start early in the week preparing my coin purse for the coming Tarzan feature. Our house was right alongside Highway 136, and I do mean right alongside. I calculate that there were maybe five feet between our front room window and the pavement, so I was cautioned to look both ways before leaving my front porch.

However, living this close to the highway was a financial boon for a young enterprising kid looking for a movie entry fee. Passing motorists were not always as ecologically attuned as they should have been, and they would throw pop bottles out the car window. After a very short time, armed with a paper sack, I could easily find at least six pop bottles that were good for a revenue of two cents each.

The cost of admission at the Bonham rose to sixteen cents when you passed the age of twelve, and that was going to put a dent in my pop bottle supply chain. I determined there must be another way around the rule, so on the first Saturday after my twelfth birthday I handed the ticket window lady twelve cents and she gave me a ticket. My smallness in stature had finally paid off. In fact, it paid off for a long time because I continued to pay twelve cents until I was sixteen. After that, I began to feel guilty. Heck, they never did ask my age at the ticket counter, so I guess I wasn't lying.

During my high school years, a second theater opened, and this one was a drive-in. The Jack Rabbit was built on a hill just off of Highway 136, about a half mile from where the highway enters the east side of town. It was a perfect place to spend a dark evening with your best girl. I don't recall what it cost to enter, but I do know that you paid by the carload and not the number of people. As a result, on many occasions, you would see kids climbing out of the trunk of the car after it was parked on the theater grounds.

The technology era had arrived in Fairbury when the Jack Rabbit opened because each car not only got its own speaker system but also a separate system that heated the car on cold Nebraska nights. When you took your girlfriend to the drive-in in the 1950s, you were doing something special.

Unlike the Bonham Theater, the Jack Rabbit had no social rules. The only social requirement was how well girlfriends and boyfriends were getting along. In one car you might see couples just watching the movie, and in other cars the windows would be totally fogged over. There were times that I wished that my windows were foggier, but I don't recall ever having a bad time at the drive-in.

There must not have been much money made by the owners of the drive-in because the Jack Rabbit did not make it through my high school days. Before I knew it, the screen, the speakers, and the heaters were gone, and a new tractor implement business was built in its place.

Movies were a way for me to escape the daily routine of being a kid. I didn't realize it at the time, but movies and news reels were my first exposure to the wonderful world beyond my present environment. Every Saturday I was getting a little smarter, and I didn't even know it. When you are having fun, learning is easy.

### Dating and Parties

Small towns presented a challenge when it came to deciding what to do or where to go on a date. Of course, there was always the movie theater and the occasional dance, but after that, you ran out of options in a hurry. I don't remember any of my friends having enough money to just take a girl out for lunch, let alone dinner. That was just unheard-of.

I think we were aware that when it came to fashion or lifestyle trends, we were at least five years behind the rest of the hip American youth. As a result, we got most of our ideas of things to do by watching movies. I recall that watching folks like Sandra Dee and Bobby Daren having fun in the sun during one of their beach blanket bingo-type movies made me want to get some of that action. However, being fifteen hundred miles from a body of water bigger than a hog trough presented a major logistics problem.

It was a problem, but not an insurmountable problem for quick-minded young men who were determined to spend a little quality time with their best girl. The Little Blue River was not quite ocean quality, but it did have some sandbars that would suffice. If the night was dark enough and you built a big enough fire and surrounded it with lots of your friends, you could have a pretty good time. Of course, it always helped if a few cases of beer showed up.

The next thing you know, people were dancing and singing and, of course, couples were sneaking off to some secluded spot down the beach to enjoy each other's company. If you let your imagination run wild, it was almost as good as the scenes from Hollywood. Beach parties were not an every-weekend thing, but they were something to look forward to and plan for. And the girls seemed to enjoy it as much as the boys did

When relationships developed to the point that "going steady" was the next logical step, a whole new avenue of dating possibilities opened up. Spending private time together seemed to be the only important thing in the world. At the time I think a lot of us looked at these serious relationships as our first and last love, and we were just around the corner from marriage and spending the rest of our lives together. Thank goodness that did not often happen.

When there was a good understanding of trust between the two date mates, the activity that got a lot of attention was "country road parking." When I say a lot of attention, I mean a lot. Like in some cases, every night.

It was not like staking out a claim, but most couples had a favorite section of a certain country road that they would occupy, and other couples would avoid the location. Oh, other couples may be parked a quarter of a mile down the road, but not in another's exact place. Some couples didn't even bother to drive to the country. They would park behind warehouses or granaries or, in one case, behind the meatpacking plant. It didn't make a difference as long as privacy was assured.

However, there were times when pranks were played on parkers. It can be very scary when strange things start happening outside your car door while you are parked in the middle of the countryside on a very dark night. Bright lights suddenly shining into the car while multiple faces stare at you through the windows can interrupt any ongoing events.

I can't speak for what happened in all the cars parked on country roads in Nebraska in the late 1950s, but for me it was pretty benign and harmless. The radio would be turned to our favorite station, most likely KOMA out of Oklahoma City. The music that would be playing would be songs like "Wake Up Little Susie," and I would spend too much time worrying that the radio would run the battery down in my excessively old car. I wasn't worried so much about the battery as I was about how we would get home and how we would explain ourselves. I should have been paying more attention to the beauty that was in the seat next to me.

There was a lot of kissing and hugging and periodic discussions of coming parties, and even an occasional reference to the distant future. I must also admit that at times there was some exploratory anatomy research that occurred. I remember being convinced that what had just happened in that country road parked car was a world-shattering event. Later I would learn that "touching" doesn't even count when it comes to world-shattering events. Never mind. It was important to me at the time.

Memories are a wonderful thing. If you listed all the activities that I partook of in my youth, and listed them by the number of times that I did them, parking on a country road with my favorite girl would probably come out number one.

**The Youth Center**

When I entered my high school days, there was one place that everyone assembled in the early evening to meet their friends and plan the rest of the night's activities. The "Youth Center" was funded by the city and was open on Wednesdays, Fridays, and Saturdays. It was operated by a young couple that must have needed the money or were just crazy enough to take the job because every night was a new adventure in keeping seventy, eighty, or a hundred young folks on the straight and narrow. We were lucky to have this facility because I do not believe that other towns that I was familiar with had a similar hangout. If you had nothing else to do, you could just stay at the youth center and play pool, play board games, or dance all evening. I know that there were some illegal or at least dastardly evil pranks developed inside the youth center, but overall it was a great way to keep kids off the streets and out of trouble.

The location of the youth center was moved once during my school years, but the original location was perfect for giving would-be trouble makers pause—the basement of the police station. You had to walk down a poorly lit alleyway and then down an outside staircase to enter the basement that the center occupied. Even as creepy as the entryway was, I don't recall any trouble developing that close to police headquarters. The center itself was just a room with pool tables and a dance floor, but to me it seemed adequate for its purpose.

Not sure why the decision was made to move the center, but my guess is that a larger and much more convenient location became available. It might even have been that the police wanted their basement back because it was very quickly converted into a shooting range.

The Elks Club had just built a new clubhouse and that left their old headquarters above the Golden Rule, a department store, wanting a tenant. The entryway to the new Youth Center was in the center of town and up some stairs from the main street, so it was perfectly located.

Additionally, the new center was much larger, with multiple rooms so that the dance floor and music was separated from all the other activities. The old Elks Club coatroom even made a perfect place for the only electronic device at the youth center, a 45 rpm record player. I never was in that room because only kids who understood the music and the artists of the day were allowed to select the music, and that was not me. I never had a record player, so as far as I was concerned, they were just a magic box.

I did enjoy dancing, and I might say that I was not too bad when it came to cutting a rug in tune with a 1950-era jitterbug. I also have great memories of slow dancing with my best girl as Elvis Presley sang "Love Me Tender." It was usually during some of those dance encounters that an agreement was reached that it was time to go park on a country road.

Whether you spent your evening at the youth center or it was just the place you started your nightly activities, most of us would end up at the bowling alley's Pla-Mor Café for something to eat before going home later that night. I didn't ever bowl because that was an expensive sport, but the bowling alley had world-famous salads, french fries, and onion rings. We usually split the bill by what each person had, so I'd make sure I had enough money at the end of the day to get my favorite chef salad. I remember the salad to not only be good but big, and that was important to a growing boy.

We would cram six or eight kids into a café booth that had been designed for four while we critiqued what had happened in the previous four- or five-hour period. This was a special time for me because as a young man who was not too sure of himself or his social status, it gave me a feeling of belonging. For a few minutes I was wedged shoulder to shoulder in a special camaraderie. This was a group that I wanted and needed to be included in. Many of them I envied for their intelligence, their athletic prowess, their good looks, and their financial independence. I needed their friendship. Listening to these friends talk about their future plans helped me build my dreams for success because I knew if they could do it, so could I.

## Jansen

About seven miles northeast of Fairbury on Highway 136 less than one hundred citizens lived in a small Jefferson County town named Jansen, Nebraska. Jefferson County has a couple of ghost towns in its inventory, but even though there were only thirty families in Jansen, it was not one of those ghost towns. Jansen had persevered since its founding in 1886 as a Mennonite sheep-herding enclave, and it had not changed much since that time. After its founding at the end of the Chicago, Rock Island and Pacific railroad spur, it grew steadily with the inclusion of a bank and other businesses until the population was about three hundred strong. Over the years, due to the loss of railway business and other agrarian issues, the population fell to the one-hundred-person level that I grew up with. But the town had not only survived; in other ways it had prospered.

What Jansen lacked in size, it made up for in character, personality, and fame. Johnny Cash would even include Jansen in his list of towns that he had visited and loved in his hit song "I've Been Everywhere." The main street of Jansen was one city block long, but the street was wide for parking. On either side of the street were the two establishments that kept Jansen famous in the 1950s—the Jansen Hotel and the Red Rooster bar. These two eating and drinking establishments were also the main reason that, as my later teen age years passed, I would spend many hours within the Jansen city limits. I have always found it interesting that a town that was established on Mennonite values of no drinking would find its place in history as one of the great little drinking towns in the west.

The Red Rooster was right on the corner of Main Street and Highway 136 and was mostly just your typical bar. I'm sure they served some food at the Rooster, but I can't recall ever eating there or having anyone tell me that they had. I do recall that there was always a jar of pickled eggs sitting on the bar, but Lord knows how long they had been there. The only vehicles parked outside the Rooster were pickup trucks that were clearly working vehicles and had probably never been washed by anything but Nebraska rain.

You kind of got the impression when entering that smoky place that you better be on your best behavior. There were always some rough-looking characters drinking at the bar, all of whom would turn and look as soon as the front door opened. The place was dark, with most of the lighting coming from the neon beer signs that covered the walls. The music that was playing on the lonely jukebox was normally of western or country content.

The bartenders were either an older lady, who had probably experienced much of Jansen's history, or a very large man with considerable girth, neither of whom had a name that I can remember. The Rooster was probably as safe as any other place in Jefferson County, but even as an adventurous young man, I was always a little leery whenever I entered. In fact, as far as I was concerned, the only reason to do business at the Red Rooster was to procure a six-pack of beer, and that was relatively easy if the fat man was on duty. He didn't seem to mind how old you were as long as you had the cash for the transaction. If the old lady was behind the bar, you might as well turn around and walk out. She was tough.

I have driven past the Rooster on several occasions in my later life, and even though I have a nostalgic urge to stop, I never have. It still looks dangerous to me.

The Jansen Hotel was the other fine town business and was located in the middle of the block on the opposite side of the street from the Rooster. The hotel was a totally different environment than the Red Rooster. The hotel not only had a bar but also served some of the finest food, mostly steaks, in the eastern part of the state. People from as far away as Omaha would venture the 130 miles on a two-lane highway just to partake of a delicious meal. Omaha had its own high-quality steak-eating establishments, but the Jansen hotel had some special credentials. There was a very fine meatpacking plant in Fairbury, only seven miles away, and the hotel received the best of the cuts of meat.

The most interesting thing about the Jansen Hotel, at least in my mind, was that there were no guest rooms. Not a single room was available to be rented out. I think there might have been a couple of rooms upstairs that the owners lived in, but there were no guest quarters. Nobody could ever explain that oddity to me, but I believe that the building was an actual hotel in Jansen's early history, and it just retained that identification through the years. But I'm guessing.

I never had the money to eat one of those delicious steaks that people were coming from far and wide to enjoy, but the hotel had another specialty that I did enjoy. The tossed salads were affordable, large, and contained lots of carrots, cheese, celery, and sliced onions, in addition to the iceberg lettuce. When this beauty of a salad was topped off with ranch dressing, you had yourself a grand meal to finish off the night. For me, it was always a toss-up as to whether the Jansen Hotel or the Pla-Mor Café had the best salad

The bar at the hotel was a lot more discreet when it came to serving liquor to minors. It fact, you had to be just plain lucky or really look old for your age if you thought you could get a beer at the hotel. However, it was worth a try on Wednesday afternoons when they had a special on draft beer for five cents a glass. That was cheaper than the twelve cents a gallon that gas was going for at the time. For a dollar you could occupy a bar stool all day, but that didn't happen to me very often.

## The CliffsNotes Of Hangouts

Hangouts may not be the best word to describe the places that I spent so many hours of my youthful years because these places and events were just a normal part of my everyday life. Every one of my hangouts taught me a little more about how to interact with people, how to communicate, and how to fit into the society of the 1950s.

When I reunite with old classmates and we discuss "the good old days," most of our discussion revolves around the various places discussed above. Listening to my classmates talk, I'm pretty sure that I was not the only one who was benefiting from the hangouts

Much of the knowledge that I absorbed as I scratched my way through a prairie childhood could not be learned in high school or college.

*The Jefferson County Courthouse, Judge Sam's lair and the centerpiece of the town square. With a city block on each side and no stoplights, it was the pivot point of cruising "the square."*

*Inspecting the kites before the competition began. This was especially important if you were competing for the work-manship or the best-looking prize. The judges needed to review the kites before they were flown because some would not survive the ordeal.*

*Lining up for photos on race day. I am driving the sleek car in the middle.*

*The makeshift ramp that was used as a starter gate for the derby race. The 2 × 4 in front of the back wheels would flip down, and the cars would commence their rapid descent down the steep track. I'm driving the car on the left.*

*This is the second model that Dad and I built. The car had a wood frame, and the metal body was made out of an old Coca-Cola sign. Dad came home very excited one day because he had found some wheels that had ball bearings—very difficult to find back then. Dad was very proud of this car.*

*All the competitors lined up for inspection before the race. Dad would closely watch the other cars and their performance to ensure that in the following years we had a car that was more streamlined.*

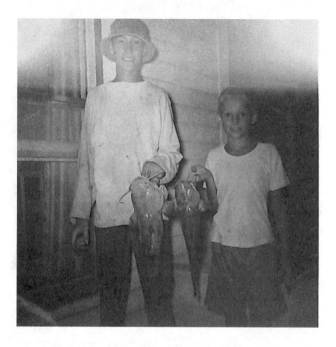

*Randy and I after a night of river fishing. We didn't break any records, but we had a lot of fun.*

*Dad in his Coca-Cola uniform. Mom always kept that uniform so clean and crisp. You would have thought he was already in the military.*

344

*The opening day of YMCA camp at Camp Jefferson. The cabin on the right is named after the Algonquian Indian tribe and is where I lived during the week. It was the closest cabin to the chow hall and the woodworking shop.*

*Brother Randy and I camping out in our backyard. We got the pup tent from a war surplus dump site just across the alleyway from our house. I think it was a five-fingered requisition. In other words, we stole it.*

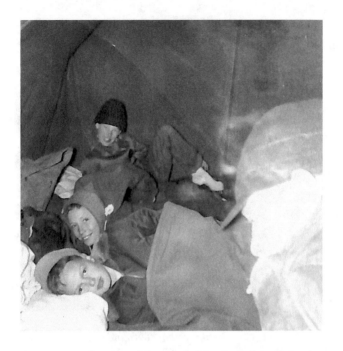

*A scout camping trip with my best friends, Bob in the back and Barry in the front. The man in the front of the photo is Judge Sam. My guess is that Sam was telling us to hold down the noise. It must have been cold that night because Bob had on his special stocking cap.*

*The scout leaders hunkered down around a campfire on a cold Nebraska night. Judge Sam is second from the left.*

*Randy and I playing our favorite game.*

*There is no painted sign or even a clue that the Red Rooster Café existed. Even though abandoned, the building still stands.*

*You can barely read the old sign that hangs over the door of the deserted Jansen Hotel. The place was hopping in the 1950s, with the best steaks in eastern Nebraska.*

*I hope the Pla-Mor Café is still serving great salads and french fries.*

*Saturday matinees at the Bonham Theater were my favor-
ite time of the week—increasing my knowledge of the world.
It pleases me that the theater has been totally renovated,
including a new marquee. However, the old marquee's rest-
ing spot was sad. I have pleasant memories of watching a
worker, on a ladder, change the title of coming attractions.*

## CHAPTER 21

## Learning How to Learn

───────────

As a kid, the word "test" caused me to shiver. As far as I was concerned, it was just a code word for failure. Failure was not an option for me, especially when being evaluated by my dad, and a test could bring failure into play. I felt like I was reasonably intelligent, but I hated to study. In my opinion, tests were designed to ferret out guys like me, to expose the fact that homework was not completed. Everybody needs a goal, and at that time in my life, mediocrity was my goal. I'm not proud of it today, but when my friend Bob was razzing me about a low test grade, taking the razzing was a manhood issue for me. I guess I thought that I was cool and that I knew just as much as he did; I just couldn't take a test. I found out later in life that I was wrong.

Fortunately, there were a whole host of teachers in my life that recognized the symptoms of a lazy kid, and they persisted in dragging me to a point in life that I changed. Looking back, I'll bet most of those teachers would have taken it as a failure if they couldn't straighten me out.

Even though I was clearly trying to avoid the effort necessary, I did have a goal in life. I knew that I had to get a college education if I was ever going to make anything of myself. Additionally, I had looked around my hometown and never saw any small-town profession that caught my fancy. I was confused, but I was too lazy to right my own ship.

For the life of me, I couldn't understand how memorizing a poem by Edgar Allan Poe or solving an algebraic equation was going to help me in any profession that I might pursue. That stubborn attitude was reason enough for me to not pay attention to homework.

And then along came Mabel.

If you wanted a picture of a person that depicted the smart, tough, tenacious, mid-1900s Midwestern teacher—you would be looking at Mabel. I don't know how long she had been teaching, but she knew every trick in the book, and a guy like me didn't have a chance. I recall that her husband was a lawyer, and I swear that she brought some of his interrogation techniques to the classroom.

Mabel taught all of the high school advanced mathematics courses, and if you wanted to eventually go to college, you had to get by Mabel first. She had me sized up from the very beginning, and I was positive that I was going to have a couple of rough years. I couldn't have been more right.

When you are sitting in a class with all your classmates who are also training for college, a lack of completed homework will expose you in a hurry. The minute I walked into her classroom, she could tell by the look in my eyes that I was arriving without the answers to last night's work. I must have looked as terrified as I was, and Mabel knew how to make me feel the heat.

Mabel had an interesting mannerism that she exhibited whenever she was very serious about a subject. When she would reach across her chest, stick her hand under her dress sleeve and pull her bra strap back up on her shoulder, you better be ready to listen. I witnessed the dreaded "bra pull" on multiple occasions as she was pointing with the other hand for me to go to the chalkboard. I was about to be embarrassed in front of all my classmates as

I struggled to pretend to know how to solve a home-work problem. There were many smirks and giggles.

This embarrassment happened so many times that I knew the routine—go to the board, take my medicine, and then crawl sheepishly back to my desk. After a few weeks of my terrible performance, I received even worse news. Mabel invited me to re-main for a while, after class was over. *Yikes*—I was going to be alone in the classroom with the chief in-terrogator. This could not be good.

When everyone else was gone from the class-room, the conversation began, and went something like this: You didn't do your homework again, did you? No, ma'am. Why not? It was too hard. Did you try? A little. Why not a lot? And then I said a real-ly dumb thing to a very smart lady: "I didn't think it was important." I could immediately see her mental antennae go up as her face got real close to mine and she pulled on her bra strap. I then got to spend the next ten minutes explaining my theory of why the Pythagorean theorem was not going to be important in my adult life. My explanation didn't even sound intelligent to me, and it was a very uncomfortable discussion.

Instead of the explosion that I deserved, Mabel just shook her head in disgust and started to talk. She was talking very slowly and precisely, so that

I would not misunderstand the importance of her message. Her treatise was not about math, but about every high school and college class that I had taken, or would take in the future. Her explanation changed my academic outlook for the rest of my life.

Mabel explained that memorizing a poem or figuring out the correct answer to a mathematical equation was important. However, there was also another equally important goal in the endeavor. The goal was to "teach a person how to think." She explained that if she were effective in only getting her students to "reason" through problems, then she considered her teaching successful. This was an amazing hallelujah moment for me. I didn't even know it before, but all along, I had been "learning how to learn."

I admit that my study habits didn't have an instantaneous turnaround after my prayer meeting with Mabel, but they did get better. I still was invited to perform at the chalkboard, but not every day, like in the past. If I started to lose focus while doing homework, I only had to think about the consequences, and I'd get right back to studying. I desperately wanted to avoid the dreaded glare and bra pull.

As my school years passed, homework didn't seem as onerous as before—I was learning how to learn.

## CHAPTER 22

## The Trip

———————

The end of a high school career brings excitement about possible college days, impending jobs, and getting away from Mom and Dad, as well as an over-all thrill of the future. However, in the case of myself and four of my friends, we were ready to put off any thought of future plans for about two weeks while we vacationed. Those two weeks in the summer following graduation have infamously become known as "the trip."

The very fact that I would get to participate in this escapade was special because I had never been very far from home. In fact, you could draw a three-hundred-mile circle around Fairbury, and you would enclose 100 percent of the territory that I was familiar with.

I'm not sure who had the original idea of the trip, but I know it wasn't me. It was probably Gerald and Art because they were the ones who owned the vehicle, a relatively new 1956 Dodge Royal, that would be used in this adventure. Besides Gerald, Art, and myself, Joe and Ed would round out the fearless five of this 1950s road trip.

With the exception of Ed, we were all members of the class of 1959 and had been friends throughout our four years together. Art, Gerald, and Ed were guys who had grown up on farms and had come to town from country schools at the beginning of our freshmen year, while Joe and I had always been "townies." The lines of where you lived had blurred over the high school years because all of us were involved in the same sports, clubs, and school activities—now we were just classmates and, best of all, we were friends.

Art was a year older than brother Gerald, but as I recall, his folks had held Art back a year so he and Gerald could attend school together. As I said, we all participated in the various high school sports programs together, but Art was a special case and a premier track athlete. When he ran, it looked al-most effortless, but the time on the stopwatch at the end of a race would indicate that he could run like the wind. In fact, even today, over fifty years later, he still holds the school record for the quarter mile. I don't have any records that I can brag about, or at least that I want out in public.

Of the five, Art was the quietest and most mild-mannered kid on the trip. I don't mean that in a disparaging way because Art did like his fun. How-ever, he would always have fun within the rules. I make the point because Art would be the one trying to keep us out of trouble during the trip, if we ever headed that way. We probably would need someone, and it certainly was not going to be me. I was the one looking for the most trouble that I could get away with.

Gerald was also a very good track man, and he could run a damn fine half mile. Additionally, like me, he could play football in an acceptable fashion, but neither of us could be considered great. I was too small, and Gerald ran funny, with his arms flailing at his side, like he was swatting flies with his elbows. I played quarterback, while he was a running back, and I got in the way of those elbows one afternoon during a practice. It must have been a day before a game because we were practicing with no pads, just running through plays. As I attempted to hand the ball off to Gerald, I caught one of his wayward right hooks to the nostrils, and I was off to the hospital with one of my several broken noses. My nose was taped, and the coach made me wear a helmet mask for the next game. I felt stupid because in those days no one ever wore a mask on their helmet. Made me feel like a wimp.

Even though they were brothers, Gerald had a completely different personality from Art, being more extroverted and in search of the good times. Living in a small town caused us to be months or even years behind the fashion scene and other worldly trends. But Gerald was the one who kept us up to date with what we should be wearing, what movies we should be watching, and what the girls should look like. Gerald was good at what he did, but we still were always months behind the trends.

For me, Gerald was the one who had the vision on where we should be headed in life, and most of the time it was to places with warmer weather, better living conditions, sophisticated drinks that I had never heard of, and expensive cigars. Gerald was cool in a lot of ways. He had the duck-tailed haircut, liked to take the girls to places that I couldn't afford, and seemed to have higher aspirations than most of us.

I envied Gerald because he was our dreamer and a very good one.

Every group needs a doer, a person who can fix anything and doesn't mind getting his hands dirty while doing it. That would be Ed. Ed had known Gerald and Art for years, having attended country schools before coming to town to complete high school. Even though Ed had graduated in the class ahead of us, he had always been a friend to all of us, and someone who should be included in the venture.

A vignette is necessary to illustrate Ed's unique ability to get things done, no matter the difficulty. Having a hot-looking car, or even a different kind of car, was something that every guy in town desired. Everyone knew that girls like guys with cool wheels. Ed had decided that the best way, and perhaps the cheapest way, to get possession of a one-of-a-kind car was to build one from the ground up. I doubt he had a mind's-eye view of what this vehicle would eventually look like because he knew it would come to him as the construction took place. The first step in Ed's car construction project was to find a well-preserved frame. But that was not a problem because there were a lot of old or abandoned cars to choose from. I don't recall what model of car he settled on for the frame, but I do remember all of us scratching our heads about how Ed would get the body removed from the frame. None of us had a crane or a chain hoist that would be necessary for the evolution. But, as usual, it didn't take Ed long to seize on the solution.

He dragged out the family torch, cut the fasteners that secured the body of the car to the frame, and warned us all to stand back. Things were getting interesting as he attached a tow rope between the soon-to-be-dismembered car body and his present operational vehicle. Jumping into his tow car, he picked up speed as he raced and pulled the helpless car around the farmyard. When he came to the end of the yard, he whipped the car around, causing the following car carcass to experience a massive amount of centrifugal force. On the second turn, the old car body exited the frame, rolled several times, and came to rest against the barn. Mission complete because, at the end of the tow rope, now sat a perfectly good frame, with axles and wheels attached. A mighty cheer went up from the rest of us, as Ed shrugged and gave us his famous "aw shucks" look. The day was complete, but I do not recall that the car was ever completed. Doesn't matter, though, because from that day forward I thought of Ed in a different way. I knew that I wanted him by my side whenever anything was broken—Ed was a fixer, and I wished I had his talent.

Try to imagine a tall, broad-shouldered, extremely virile-looking high school football tight end and that would be Joe. Back then, I didn't know what virile meant, but today I know that is what Joe was. If you were going to be a smart-mouth around some bad people, and I sometimes was, Joe was the guy that you wanted standing next to you because his size could be intimidating. But, in spite of all his masculine presence, Joe was a gentle giant who spoke softly and always had a calm smile.

In preparation for taking the field before football games, the rest of the team would stand back as the coach would get in Joe's face and try to convince him that it would be OK to go out and hurt someone. You could almost sense that the coach wanted to slap him around a little, just to make him mad, but he didn't. Joe was just a nice guy.

The only time that I ever saw Joe angered was on a summer evening when Joe and I had driven the twenty miles to Kansas to get some beer. Because Kansas was a state that allowed eighteen-year-olds to drink beer and Nebraska was a twenty-one state, we had made this trip on various occasions. However, that night's planned trip was going to be special because of two nice-looking young ladies who lived in Mahaska, Kansas.

Little did we know that while we were enjoying ourselves over a 3.2 percent beer and some friendly female companionship, the word of our presence had gotten around to the young men of Mahaska. Three of these boys decided that Joe and I had overstepped our bounds by invading their territory and that there should be retribution.

The town couldn't have had a population of more than fifty, and there was only one street, but the young men of Mahaska were always fit from working the fields, so if there was to be a fight, it could get ugly. As we left the local drinking establishment, we had a few words with the angry mob, but it didn't sound serious, and we proceeded to the car. As usual, Joe was very low-key about the whole affair, and we were joking and laughing as we drove down the main street to exit the hostile zone.

Just then, one of those boys lost his head and launched a beer bottle that struck the car, causing Joe to slam on the brakes and exit the car in a manner that I had not seen before from the gentle giant. As I came from the other side of the car, the scene before me was like one out of the movie *High Noon*. Three angry town protectors at one end of the street, and Joe and I at the other end. I was glad to see Joe's fists clenched and shoulders hunched because my assessment was that Joe would have to take two of them, and I would do the best I could with the other until he arrived. It was good to stand next to an angry giant! I remember thinking about the fact that my mother was born in Mahaska and my grandfather lived about two miles from where I now stood. If there was to be a fight, my family would know about it before the sun came up, and then I would be in trouble, in more ways than one.

Bad language and insults were hurled back and forth as we approached each other. But as we got closer, it became clear that the Mahaska boys' hearts were not in this fight. After a few minutes of both groups glaring at each other, the hometown boy's evaluation of a very upset Joe was proper, and they backed down. It was a good decision for them, and probably for me because I would have gotten roughed up a bit. I never saw Joe that mad again, ever, but I was happy to see it that night.

Looking back on this band of friends, I find it interesting that as much time as we were together during our school years, I do not recall that we spent time at each other's homes. I never was in Ed's or Joe's home, and they were never in mine. To my knowledge, Art and Gerald were only in my home once or twice. I do remember Gerald being in my house the night that I rolled my dad's car. It just didn't seem important that we knew how each other lived at home or what our parents were like, but I do remember one visit to Gerald and Art's farm because it stirred the history buff in me.

History books will tell you that millions of years ago Nebraska was covered in ocean-type waters and marshlands, lands and seas that were roamed by pre-historic dinosaurs of all shapes and sizes. Erosion of soil in one of Gerald and Art's farm fields revealed an almost totally complete, well-preserved skeleton of one of these ancient critters, and I was enthralled just looking at it. It was like having a museum in the backyard. I do believe that the relic had been offered up for restoration and viewing at the university museum, but the offer had been refused. It seems that most Nebraska farmers had a similar skeleton in their fields and the university could handle only so many old bones. That skeleton is probably still sticking out of Jefferson County soil.

As the day of departure on our trip approached, I remember being excited, but I do not recall much advance preparation. Like the other guys, I evaluated how much money I had for the trip while I subconsciously calculated how much of a dent this trip was going to put in my college fund. The plan was to share all the expenses, and I was sure that even I could handle my end of the cost of five guys in one motel room. Even though the plan was to take turns sleeping on the only bed in the room, I didn't care if I slept on the floor every night, and I bet the other guys felt the same way. I set aside the amount of money that I felt would be my share for gas and lodging, subtracted it from my total, and the remainder was for fun. I knew that I had enough to make it because fun was the primary mission.

There wasn't a lot of luggage involved because we were determined to spend the entire trip in shorts, T-shirts, and tennis shoes. However, I'm glad I also took jeans and my high school letter jacket along because we had some cold nights, even in August.

On the opening day of the adventure, Gerald and Art arrived with a gassed-up and freshly washed and vacuumed Dodge, and the rest of us threw a small duffel bag of clean underwear and such into the trunk. As we all piled in, Ed announced that during his trip preparation he had procured a sizable quantity of rum-soaked crook cigars for our enjoyment along the way. At the time, I thought, *Good for Ed and good for us*, because this trip is all about girls, drinking beer, smoking cigars, and did I mention girls. Those cigars probably only cost a nickel each, but the way I saw it, Joe and I couldn't afford a nickel, Art was too good a guy to smoke any kind of cigar, and it was beneath Gerald's dignity to buy a cigar that cost less than fifty cents, so my intention was to enjoy these freebies. Little did I know then that before the trip was over I would learn to hate the smell of rum-soaked cigars.

The exodus began with high hopes as we headed west on Highway 36. The original plan had been to transit the full length of southern Nebraska before shooting across the Colorado line, straight for Boulder, but I had a personal plan that I was hoping to spring on the guys. I remember those first few hours as an exhilarating time, with the AM radio blaring out tunes like "Lipstick on Your Collar" and "Pink Shoe Laces," and then the scramble to find the next audible station as we traveled out of AM range of each small town. We knew that if we were still driving into the evening that we would be able to get KOMA out of Oklahoma City, and KOMA had the best music in the entire Midwest.

With five guys in the car, there was constant chatter about girls and our high hopes of meeting every young female on our trail. As this discussion progressed, I found an opening for my idea that maybe we should alter our travel plan and head a little northwest to Grant, Nebraska, for a short visit to lovely Linda.

The guys all knew Linda because even though she lived in Grant, she periodically visited her sister, who lived in Fairbury. Her visits to her sister were normally during the summer months, and because I was the only guy in the car who had dated Linda, I can tell you that she could turn a warm day into a real sizzler. I always thought she looked like Elizabeth Taylor, and when I looked at her, all I could think of was *Cat on a Hot Tin Roof*. It was always a good summer when Linda visited.

None of the guys were too excited about my idea because they could see that there was some personal gratification on my mind, so I had to do some fast talking. I reasoned that Grant really was not that far off the original travel path and that we had been driving a long time and we needed to stretch our legs. Besides, Art was complaining about the rum-smelling cigar smoke, and Grant would be a good place to air out the car.

I think I was making progress in winning over converts for my plan when suddenly the worst thing that can happen to cash-strapped travelers happened. The dash of the Dodge lit up in red, and Art announced that there would be no trip to Grant and that we needed to find a mechanic, fast. Fortunately, we were fairly close to the major town of McCook, so as we limped into town with the generator light a brilliant color, we were focused on finding the first reputable-looking automobile shop. I do not recall how that repair was paid for, but I know that it put a dent in our resources and a damper on the trip's beginning. It also destroyed any argument that I had for visiting lovely Linda. Young loves pass quickly and I was just fine with what happened, once we were on the road again.

Because of our repair delay, it was decided that making it to Boulder that day was out of the question unless we wanted to drive really late, and no one did. Because of a little preplanning on my part, Fort Morgan, which was right on our chosen path, was selected as an excellent place to spend the first night. Earlier in the year I had made contact with Colene, who was now living in Fort Morgan, and warned her that we might stop by sometime in the summer for a little visit. As you might recall, Colene was my pretty redheaded girlfriend in kindergarten. I had managed to keep track of her, even when she moved away from town. Her father had been the owner or manager or something big at the Fairbury airport, and I always thought he had the best job in town. I suspect that he moved out west because of a better offer with a bigger airport, but I'm just guessing. Fairbury's airport was pretty small. Anyway, if we could just walk in, unannounced, on Colene's family, we might be able to get a free night's lodging, and that would help us recover a little from our generator expense. It was worth a try, so all of us except Art lit up a cigar, turned the radio up to its maximum level, and continued west. Even though Art didn't like the noise, "Wake Up Little Susie" was coming in loud and clear.

Our arrival at Colene's house was well timed to coincide with dinner, and even though her folks were surprised, they pretended to be happy to see us. After a lot of hugs and chit-chat, Colene's mother disappeared into the kitchen to resupply the table because all day on the road had produced five hungry teenagers. That evening was spent relaxing and telling travel stories, as if we had been on the road for two weeks already.

Colorado is an eighteen-year-old drinking state, and I kept hoping that Colene's dad would offer us a beer, but that didn't happen. Probably just as well because we were all ready to hit the sack fairly early.

Her mother went into the protective mother quail mode and decided that all five of us should sleep in the basement family room, far away from her beautiful young daughter. It certainly was not necessary to separate us with a locked door, but it was probably a good idea overall. You don't want five road-dirty, rum-crook-breathing, intestinally challenged teens sleeping on your best living room furniture.

The next day found us well rested, and after a hearty breakfast, we left my pretty redheaded kindergarten girlfriend in the rearview mirror and headed off to the mother of all parties, Boulder, Colorado. It may still be this way today, but in 1959 the University of Colorado was known as one of the top party schools in the country, and it was one of those schools that I would have loved to attend.

Today I know that attending a school because of party status is a really dumb idea, but when you are young, your priorities can be confused. I was not alone with Boulder being on my academic bucket list because most of what I knew about the university I learned from Gerald. Even thinking about Colorado could be dangerous territory for a young Cornhusker because there was a substantial amount of athletic competition between the two states. However, my guess is that all five of us were thinking the same thing as we pulled into town—*We love Boulder* and *Let's find the girls and the beer*. The first task of finding a motel that would take all of us in one room, at the right price, was accomplished in short order, and then we were off to see the campus. Our source of all sophisticated knowledge, Gerald, informed us that a must-see was a bar located just off campus called The Sink. I have no idea how Gerald knew these things, but I trusted his recommendations. As I've said before, Gerald was cool.

Our excitement was building when we found The Sink because the place was crawling with thirsty undergraduates. This was no ordinary hole-in-the-wall, and it could be better described as a hole-in-the-ground because to enter, you needed to walk down a staircase into a basement-like room. The smell of that stairwell reminded me a little of the aromas found down on the farm, but it did not deter us from crawling up to an even dirtier table for a few beers. Perhaps this place was mislabeled and should have been named after another bathroom appliance.

Looking around the room, it was hard to see more than a few tables away because it was so dark, but you could tell by the laughter that folks were having fun. I overheard one discussion that indicated that the speaker should be in class instead of underground. I could hardly wait to start college so I could say those kinds of cool things. It was difficult to make out the specifics of the artwork on the wall, but every inch of wall space was covered with pictures of grotesque creatures who were tearing out their own intestines. I don't think we had anything to eat.

Our day of acting like college guys was one that we would not soon forget, but there was some disappointment in the fact that we could not claim one new female acquaintance.

After a couple of days in Boulder doing nothing but walking around and viewing the sights, it was time to move on. The entire stay in that city was a replication of our single night at The Sink. We still had no new female friends. Even though Gerald tried to tutor us, I don't think the Colorado girls were ready for us country boys.

Just west of Denver, on the initial climb up the Rockies, is the wonderful town of Golden, Colorado, and this had been one of our planned destinations from the very start. Golden is very close to Lookout Mountain, where Buffalo Bill is buried, but I don't remember that we visited his grave. However, every teenager in the Midwest knew that Golden was the home of the Coors Brewery, and this was a must-see for five guys who were out to see the world. Coors today is a nationally recognized beverage, but in 1959 it was only sold in ten Midwestern states. Coors' claim to fame was that it was made with the purest and freshest Rocky Mountain water, so the taste must be wonderful, and of course this was believed by every customer that bought the beer.

For some reason, I don't recall why, we decided not to take the brewery tour. Looking back, this was a strange decision because that visit had been the subject of many discussions over the previous months. Maybe we noticed that there were no girls in the waiting line, and, therefore, the tour was wasted energy—who knows?

But we did know that we couldn't go back to Fairbury without some kind of exciting story about our visit to Golden, so the wheels of mischief were spinning. It doesn't matter who initially came up with the idea, even though it was probably me, but in a four-to-one vote we decided to leave our mark on this famous town. After looking at a local map, we found the road that ran alongside Clear Creek, the source of that fresh Rocky Mountain water. With Art at the wheel of the Dodge, but complaining about possible legal problems, we followed that road until we found a scenic parking place where we could walk down to the fast-moving river. On that very spot, on that day in August 1959, five Jefferson County, Nebraska boys peed in a Jefferson County, Colorado river, contaminating a national icon forever. Every time I see Coors beer on a store shelf, I smile.

Before we left the eastern slope of the Rocky Mountains and crossed the Great Divide, we decided to take in an amusement park in Loveland. After all, the park was right off of Highway 34, and that was the road that we were going to take as we headed west, up the Big Thompson Canyon toward Estes Park. There was also some discussion that a warm summer day in an amusement park was a good place to see girls wearing shorts, so the vote for the park stop was five to zero.

One of the guys had done some research because I remember being lectured about the fact that the park's main attraction was a roller coaster named the Cyclone. I have never been very keen on riding roller coasters, and as the years have gone by, I avoid them altogether. Even as a kid, they did not look safe to me, and as an adult, with some engineering background, they look downright dangerous.

That night I earned the reputation as the class chicken, and maybe a few other names, because four guys rode the monster rollercoaster, and I did not. The Cyclone was not really old—it had been built in 1940—but that thing was made of wood, and it creaked as the cars raced around its track and out over the lake. There was no way I was getting on that thing. I'm told that that rickety old ride still operates today, some fifty-five years later. I guess it must be safe.

We finished off the evening by buying a six-pack of Coors and drinking it while we watched the park revelers walk by. We were not as big a party group as we thought we were because we ended up throwing two of the beers away before we went to bed. I'll blame Art for that because he didn't help drink the stuff. But the worst disappointment was that we, again, met no girls. Maybe our luck would change on the other side of the Rockies.

There had never really been any plans for where we would go after we left Colorado, but there was a universal agreement that we should keep moving west. We started the Rocky Mountain climb, up through the Big Thompson Canyon toward Estes Park, with the radio blaring the latest tunes, like "Rock Around the Clock" and "The Three Bells." The town of Estes Park was one of our first stops, and I know the small-town boy in me was showing as we walked the streets. To me, this was one of those tourist towns that I had only seen in the movies. People from every state were enjoying the sights and obviously spending more money than I could imagine. I felt like a big deal, just being in the same place as all these other travelers.

The altitude of the highway continued to increase as we entered the Rocky Mountain National Park and transited on the highest paved, continuously operated road in America. Trail Ridge Road is one of those national assets that everyone should see at least once, but you need to do it in the summer because it is not open during the winter months. As we traveled, we marveled that there could be as much as eight feet of snow on either side of the road in June. The snowplows would literally tunnel through the snow as they attempted to keep the roads clear. I was amazed as we ascended above the tree line.

The tree line looks well defined from a distance, but up close you can see that the diminishing line of trees is gradual as the altitude increases. The trees are stunted and small because they cannot survive in certain harsh conditions. After a zone of stunted trees, there are none at all.

When we reached the maximum height of the road and crossed the Continental Divide, well above twelve thousand feet, we found that we could still have an August snowball fight, and so we did. The fight didn't last long, though, because we were all panting from the lack of oxygen.

Years later I would read that Trail Ridge Road followed the actual path that the Arapahoe and Ute Indians would travel from their homes in the west to the hunting grounds in the east. It must have been a heck of a walk. The story that I read said that the name they gave the trail was "Taienbaa," which meant "where the children walk." It seems that the trail was so steep that the parents couldn't carry the children anymore, so they put them down and told them to walk or die.

The Dodge was running fine, and it had been working hard through the steep and winding road of the mountain climb, but conditions were about to change. As the front end of that car pointed downhill on the western side of the Rockies, Art shifted to the lowest transmission gear, and we started our descent. I doubt that the accelerator was touched again until we were on the flatland, west of the mountains.

As the trip continued west, we were now in a whole new territory for me. I didn't want to admit it to the other guys, but I was as far from home as I had ever been. Not sure how to explain it, but just seeing the new and different countryside pass the window was exciting to me.

I hadn't been to a lot of cities in my life, but every one that I had seen seemed to be a relatively dirty place. Maybe that's why my initial impression of Salt Lake City was so different. You just didn't see debris in the streets, and if there was debris, there was someone there cleaning it up. Additionally, the town was much quieter than you would expect from a large population. As I now know, I was easily impressed in those days, but my memory of Salt Lake City is that this was a safe and easy city to live in.

There were two major reasons that we had decided to come to this area, and they both had to do with salt. Even in Nebraska, you could not have a 1950s childhood without hearing about Craig Breedlove, Donald Campbell, and John Cobb attempting to break the land speed record on the Utah salt flats. At the time, everyone was trying to break Cobb's record by traveling over four hundred miles per hour, and we wanted to see what the flats really looked like. Turns out, it was kind of boring, just a bunch of salt. And on a hot August day, a white desert of salt was not a good place to be. We checked the flats off our "to-see list" and moved on down the road.

The second salt phenomenon was a little more dramatic, but the Great Salt Lake itself was also a bit uncomfortable. You could not come all this way without taking a dip in the lake, even though it looked and smelled like the unnatural thing to do. It was surreal to see the swimmers, floating on their backs but barely submerged in the water. Their bodies seemed to hover above the water, and not the way you would normally see them float. Undeterred, we had to try it, but I did not last long. Ed and Joe stayed in longer than the rest of us, just to prove how tough they were. As far as I was concerned, they could win that contest. The salty water in that lake must have some redeeming medical qualities, though, because Ed claimed that after his swim, he never again suffered from athlete's foot.

After a little more time in the city, and then on to Ogden, Utah, for what reason I cannot say, it was time to figure out where our next major stop would be. As we evaluated our Utah time, it was clear that we again failed in some of our primary mission. We were leaving the state after drinking no beer, because it was against the law, and no new female names were in our little black books. I must admit that I was becoming disappointed and a little irritable about the results of the trip so far.

Gerald led the powwow of decision making about the next stop because he had a personal goal in mind. He made a strong case for heading to California so that we could see the Pacific Ocean, palm trees, and movie stars. But there was a hidden agenda on Gerald's mind that we were to soon learn about. We had overlooked the fact that earlier in the summer Gerald had met a pretty young California girl who was visiting relatives in Fairbury. We had all met her, but Gerald was the only one who had the nerve to ask her for a date. I say pretty, but she was actually beautiful, and of course she had that West Coast aura that country boys could not overlook.

I can't recall her name, but I do remember that she was from San Gabriel or one of those other California towns with a fancy name. The truth is always a little fuzzy when you are trying to impress someone, but she had told Gerald that she was a Rose Bowl princess, and that was too much fame for him to overlook. So, I could understand why he was going to keep pushing for a California destination.

Perhaps we made a mistake, but common sense overtook us, and in the end California was deleted from the itinerary. A closer calculation indicated that funds were running low, and we needed to choose a less costly destination. I wanted to see that ocean, but I was OK with the decision because I had started off the trip with a smaller bank account than the rest.

After a cursory look at the map, Yellowstone Park was chosen to host our next event. With high expectations we sped on down the road while smoking some of the remaining rum crooks and listening to Connie Francis sing "Mary Lou."

After a certain number of days on the road, crammed into a small space, five friends became five sweaty bodies, and we started to wear on each other. Oh, I don't mean like in a hostile way, but the bickering had taken on a life of its own. Finally, Art, who had been the chaperone from the beginning, was fed up and decided to take remedial action. The brakes screeched, and the Dodge left the paved surface and came to a stop on the grassy side of the road. Art announced that everybody was to get out of the car and resolve the situation. With that, somewhere along Highway 15 in Utah, four suntanned bodies rolled into the ditch to finish the issue. I can't remember what the actual issue was, so it was probably just being cooped up for so long.

If there was to be a fight, this was going to be a short one because we all knew that Joe was going to win. There was no reason to fight. After a few short seconds of rolling in the grass, it was over, and we laid there, looking up at the sky and laughing. With the tension broken, and the relaxed feeling of being out of the car for a while, our discussion turned again to the fairer sex. We were sure that our luck would improve when we got to Yellowstone because we had heard the stories of the young guys and gals that spend the summers working in the restaurants and hotels in the park. There was bound to be some girls who would like to party with five good-looking guys.

As we transited across Wyoming and passed the Grand Tetons, we laughed a lot about how the mountains got their name. Boys will be boys, you know.

When we approached the south gate of Yellowstone, we started looking for a place to stay because it was getting late in the afternoon and we didn't know what might be available in the park. We started seeing roadside signs advertising a dude ranch that championed itself as the last accommodations before entering the park. It did not take us long to agree that staying at a dude ranch would be a neat story to tell when we returned home, so we entered the gate to Flagg Ranch and started one of the best days of our trip

The very good-looking girl who served us an early dinner was not only nice to us, she was a vast source of local knowledge. Finally, we had hit the jackpot. Flagg Ranch had its own dormitory full of young employees, and we were talking dozens and dozens of females.

We ate much faster when the young lady agreed that she and her girlfriends should meet us, after they got off work, later in the evening. We had no idea how many other girls we were talking about, or what they were going to look like, but I don't recall even worrying about the matter. The game was on, and that is all we cared about. The trip was suddenly becoming more fun.

After a quick shower and a lot of banter about the upcoming event, we bought some beer and anxiously waited for the girls to arrive. We were not disappointed upon their arrival because the five girls turned out to be pleasant to the eye and, more importantly, seemed to be ready to enjoy the evening. In fact, because we had no idea what there was to do, the girls were proactive in the discussion of how we should spend our date night. They declared that because of the full moon and the coolness of the night, it would be a great time to go skinny-dipping in one of the hot springs. Now, we guys had not even been in the park yet, but we knew that swimming in the hot springs was against the law, and we were not prepared to go to jail, no matter how pretty the girls were. I'm sure we sounded a little rural and prudish as we tried to back away from the hot springs discussion, even though I was dreaming of how much fun it would be.

The girls wouldn't let go of the idea, and being the silver-tongued devils that they were, we started to relent. I knew that I was ready to vote when they informed us that the hot springs in question were actually just outside the park boundary, and, therefore, in a legal zone. I have no idea if it was true or not, but when I saw the other guys' heads nodding up and down in agreement, I was ready to go.

It wasn't a very long car ride before we were suddenly in the middle of a field, and in the bright moonlight you could see steam rising out of the ground. There were no swimsuits involved, so some wore underwear and others a birthday suit, which was very exciting for the five of us.

At one end of this bubbling pool the water was at the temperature of hot tubs that I would enjoy later in life. However, you didn't want to move to the end where the water was actually bubbling out of the ground. I'd like to report that we drank a lot of beer and got wild and crazy, but that did not happen. We all sat in the moonlight, bathed in the hot water, smelled the sulfur aroma of the steam, talked and giggled a lot.

After a while, a head count indicated that two bodies were missing, but there was enough light that we could see movement in the back seat of the Dodge. Ed and Myrna had decided that a little privacy was exactly what they needed. There was at least a whole lot of kissy face going on. Later, we would tease Ed, but he swore that he and Myrna were just having a little harmless fun. Only those two will ever know, but one thing is for sure. Myrna is the only girl's name that could be recalled, fifty years after the fact.

When it was time to depart, there was a frenzy over the lack of towels as ten youngsters tried to dry off. Wiggling out of wet underwear on a chilly Wyoming night brought more laughter as Ed's farmer-tanned white butt shone in the moonlight, but he didn't seem to care. As the evening ended, I realized that after so many days on the road, it was the first time we had met all of our objectives—girls, beer, and fun. I slept well that night.

Yellowstone is known mainly for its natural beauty and, of course, its hot springs and the mother of all geysers, Old Faithful. In addition, travelers should not underestimate the number of wild creatures that can be seen running free as you drive through the park. Hardly a day passes that you don't see deer, moose, elk, and, of course, bear grazing close to the road, while bald eagles soar overhead.

I'm sure this is spectacular for everyone, but for me it was only something that I had dreamed of. Every river and stream that we passed I had the urge to jump out of the car and throw a fishing line in the water because I knew there were large trout waiting to be hooked. I think I was the only wanna-be fisherman in the car, so my urge remained a dream.

Vacationers are not always the smartest folks on the road, and we witnessed some events that indicated that adult supervision should have been present. On multiple occasions, cars would be backed up on the road in what was referred to as a "bear jam." Usually this was caused by one or more mother bears and a collection of cubs that had decided to have playtime on the centerline of the highway. Drivers didn't mind the delay because it gave their families the opportunity to stretch their legs, and best of all, to get up close and personal with the bears. The problem was that some folks lost sight of the fact that these are wild animals and you need to stay well clear of them. We saw mothers sitting their small children close to the bears so they could get a scrapbook photo, which even five teenage boys thought was stupid. We watched and waited for a terrible disaster when we saw a father actually trying to sit a child on a bear for a picture. Fortunately, the wooly mammoth ran away.

Moose are another animal that should not be trusted at short range because they are much larger than I had imagined and they have a very grumpy personality. I learned that at a "moose jam" one does not get out of the car and one does not aggravate the moose. The lead car in one backup was a Volkswagen Beetle, driven by an intense lady who was in a big hurry. The moose was giving her an equally intense look as she continued to honk at the giant, but he was not moving. When the honking had no effect, she decided to pull up and just bump the animal in an effort to budge him from the road. That was clearly not the right thing to do because the moose turned his oversized antlers on the VW and used his huge weight advantage to turn the car on its side. When the deed was done, the moose left, and the only injury was to the wee car. What a great day; we were seeing so many cool things!

Fishing Bridge was a campground and lodge area at the north end of Lake Yellowstone, and it became the place that we would stay and operate out of during our visit. It was perfect because Fishing Bridge was centrally situated in the park and a relatively short driving distance from all the sights.

Additionally, there was a large colony of young workers at the lodge, which gave us hope for a Flagg Ranch repeat.

The cabin that we stayed in was not very big, being only one room, but it was adequate. By this time in the trip, we were all used to sleeping on the floor anyway. I'm not sure why, but all the cabins were built on stilts, about three feet tall, so you could look right under the cabin, from front to back. It looked like they were expecting high water, but that couldn't be, up here in the mountains. Guess I should have asked.

One day at breakfast we chatted with a ranger who explained to us that his job was in the area of bear removal. Turns out that the bears that we had seen to that point were smaller black bears, which the park supervisors were not too concerned with. However, when a large grizzly would come out of the wilderness to scare the picnickers, the ranger and his buddies would spring into action. Their job was to capture the oversized eating machine and haul him back up into the mountains for release. Our eyes must have been wide with excitement as we listened to him describe his neat job because he asked if we had seen a grizzly yet. Answering no, he offered up that if we wanted to meet him later that night, he might be able to give us a close-up look at a big fellow. We were all in!

We met the ranger that evening, and while piling into his truck, he instructed us to keep the windows up at all times. It was getting very dark when we arrived at what he informed us was the central campsite garbage dump. What I could make out in the very dim light was a number of fifty-five gallon barrels, which I assumed were full of refuse, sitting in a large empty lot. The ranger parked the truck about thirty yards from the barrels, with the front end of the truck pointing at the main cluster of containers. With the truck lights off and the darkness becoming even more opaque, we sat and chatted quietly, not knowing exactly what was about to happen.

After about an hour, the ranger informed us that it was time for some excitement, and that we should look straight out the windshield because he was about to hit the lights. As the big truck's lights illuminated the area, five teenage mouths dropped open and a unison utterance of "Wow" issued forth. There, just a few yards in front of us, was a huge brown, wooly grizzly, standing on his hind legs over an open barrel. It is hard to explain how big he appeared, but at the time, it looked like that fifty-five-gallon container was as small as a beer can. I kept thinking about the ranger's stupid order to keep the windows rolled up. If that bear wanted in that truck, no windows were going to stop him, but the windows stayed up. It was good that our new acquaintance was not looking for trouble. The bear just looked directly into the lights, let out a low-key growl, pushed the barrel over, and slowly ambled out of our sight. The ranger laughed and said that he and the other rangers in the group would be back the next night to give the animal a ride. I couldn't imagine our trip getting any more exciting, but I was about to find out how wrong I could be.

Late one evening, after a long night of searching out the young girls, the five of us got ready to settle down for a good sleep. As usual, there was only one bed in the cabin, so four of us were preparing our nests at various places around the cabin floor. I had chosen the area between the bed and the wall, in hopes that I wouldn't get stepped on during the many visits to the bathroom. Joe decided that he wasn't yet ready to sleep, so he went outside to the car to get a transistor radio that he hoped still had some battery power. Casey Kasem would undoubtedly have our favorite tunes spinning through the airways.

Shortly after Joe left the cabin and closed the door, the excitement began. The cabin started swaying at such a rate that it threw me under the bed and then out again into the wall. The single lightbulb that hung from a cord in the middle of the room was doing a great impression of a long pendulum. Between the shaking of the room and the shadows on the walls, and the many "What the hells" being yelled, we knew we had a serious situation. The first diagnosis by all of us was that there was a big bear under the cabin and the stilted edifice was about to come down.

The next thought was *Crap, Joe is outside, and he'll get eaten*. Joe would tell us later that he had just opened the car door and started to reach under the seat for the radio when the car started to shake, so he jumped in, closed the door, and hunkered down. He thought that a bear was pushing the car around. Clearly, we were all psyched from the night with the ranger.

When the initial rock-and-roll act was over, we went outside to search for Joe, hoping that we wouldn't find him in pieces. We were not alone because everyone at Fishing Bridge, and my guess, for miles around, was standing under the stars wondering the same thing. It would only be after a long night of mini shakes that we would find out what we had been part of.

The 11:37 p.m. earthquake on August 17, 1959, turned out to be one of the strongest ever recorded in the northwest of the United States, registering 7.5 on the Richter magnitude scale. The epicenter of the quake was only about twenty miles from where we were bedded down for the night, and the quake could be felt all the way to Salt Lake City.

The landscape around the center of the quake dropped twenty feet, and the shake caused the most land and mud slides in the history of the country since 1927. History would record that eighty million tons of rock, mud, and debris would flow into the Madison River Valley, and hurricane force winds that tossed cars into the air were recorded. This slide alone damned the river, causing the creation of "Quake Lake." The statistics of this event were staggering, but the most devastating was that hundreds of people were hurt and twenty-eight died.

The five of us were OK, but as the sun came up, we realized that this was not going to be a normal day in the park. Roads in and around Yellowstone were blocked because of rock slides, and in places the road had heaved up, like there had been a subterranean explosion. Additionally, most of the communication capability from the park had been wiped out.

I don't remember any of us really worrying about what was going on, and because we were just fine, we watched and enjoyed being part of history. After a while, though, Art reminded us that folks back home might be interested in our well-being. That started a two-day vigil in a phone booth, trying to get a line out and hoping that someone at the other end of the line would pick up. For hours and hours on end we would take turns placing calls, but it was clear that we were not going to succeed, so by a vote of five to zero we decided to start our trek home. It would not be until we had gone two hundred miles across Wyoming that I would be able to place a call to my boss at the municipal swimming pool and give him a status report that he could pass on to our families. News traveled slowly in those days, as witnessed by the fact that Fairbury hadn't even heard that there had been a quake. We were premature in thinking that anyone was worried about us, or even cared.

As our great exodus drew to a close, and we traveled across the great, empty, but beautiful space of Wyoming and western Nebraska, we laughed and reviewed our many adventures. We smoked the last of Ed's cigars and made fun of his episode with Myrna. We made fun of Joe's bear retreat into the car. We chided Gerald because he was still upset about not going to California. We teased Art for being our mother hen and chaperone. And I took a lot of heat for pretrip bragging and then drinking such a small amount of beer and not finding any female companionship.

As the 1956 Dodge roared across the prairie, and the radio blasted out "Blue Suede Shoes" and other Elvis Presley hits, I was convinced that this was the best that life could be, and maybe it was.

All five of us went our separate ways in life, and we all had successful careers. But each time we would meet during the succeeding years, we would relish the opportunity to relive the stories of our trip. I must tell you, the tales got better and better every time they were told.

*Gerald is on the right, and Art is in the middle. This photo was taken in my mom and dad's small front room. If Gerald had stretched out his left arm and I had stretched out my right, we could have touched both walls of the room.*

*From left to right: Ed, Joe, Gerald, and me. Even in August, on top of Trail Ridge Road, it was good that we had brought our letter jackets. It was cold, and the snow was perfect for a snowball fight.*

*Joe is on the left, and Art is on the right, as we observe the hot and dry Great Salt Lake. This was not the most fun swim I've ever had.*

## CHAPTER 23

## Stroke of Luck

———————

As I was trying to find my way in life, I attended one year at Fairbury Junior College—it no longer exists—and then a year at the University of Nebraska. However, I had very little to show for my effort. My grades had not been particularly good, and I was struggling to figure out what I should major in. It was difficult for me to decide what to study when I didn't know what I wanted to do with my life.

One Friday night, late in my sophomore year, I was stopped by a Lincoln police officer for speeding, but he only gave me a warning and sent me on my way. The officer's good will was a huge relief for at least two reasons. At the end of the school year I was totally out of cash, and especially out of money to pay for a ticket. Secondly, with my already bad grades, I didn't need my folks finding out that I was also goofing off. As I proceeded back to the dormitory on campus, I put the police interaction out of my mind. I was at school, seventy miles from my parent's house, and there was no reason to believe that the jungle drums were so good that Mom and Dad would ever hear about it. I slept well that night.

The following morning I was awakened with a message that I had a telephone call on the corridor phone. I trudged down the hall in my underwear to answer the phone, only to hear my dad's voice say, "What have you been up to?" My mind raced to figure out how to answer the question, but I couldn't get past the bigger issue of how he had found out about the police incident so fast. Sweat was running off my forehead, and I started to mumble when he hit me with the next phrase—"I've got a letter here." How could he have a letter? There was no such thing as overnight delivery.

It is a good thing that no words were coming out of my mouth, and that he couldn't see my face, because I was in panic mode. He saved me by finally saying, "This letter says that you have been accepted at the United States Naval Academy in Annapolis, Maryland."

From that moment on, my life changed forever. Fate had chosen my career for me.

*Boarding the plane in Omaha, bound for Friendship
Airport in Baltimore, Maryland (now BWI), and then on to
Annapolis. Little did I know that thirty-seven years later, I
would retire from the US Navy in Omaha.*

*Small world.*

## Epilogue

My thirty-seven years of wearing the cloth of my country were filled with adventure, excitement, boredom, and times of enormous stress and responsibility. My warfare specialty was in the nuclear submarine force, and I was privileged to be trained in the program headed up by Admiral Hyman Rickover, the father of the nuclear navy.

I served on multiple submarines and then was honored to command the nuclear attack submarine, USS *Birmingham* (SSN 695). My ascent through the ranks and my command tour took place during the height of the Cold War, so there was a lot of interaction going on, above and under the sea. In my biased and personal opinion, commanding a submarine is the last outpost of responsibility. There is no one to turn to when things don't go as planned, and they never do. Communications in those days were barely minimal, and some of us actually pulled the fuses on our radios so that we couldn't inadvertently transmit and give away the ship's position. When headquarters sent you messages, they just assumed that you got them because you did not acknowledge.

Deployments were lengthy and more difficult for the families than they were for those of us aboard the ship. With no communications, the first time your boss and your family would hear from you is when you popped up just off of your home port coast, months after you left. Sadly, there was one time when a crew's family was waiting on the pier and the ship did not come back. Very sad, and I lost friends.

These were serious times, and very heady times, for a young naval officer who had grown up in dusty fields and on the streets of a small Midwestern town. At times I would look in the mirror and marvel that my country would trust me with a ship that cost over two billion dollars—trusted me with the safe operation of a nuclear reactor and, of course, special weapons that could cause enormous damage, if the leadership of the country chose to use them.

But the heaviest load of responsibility was that my country trusted me with the safety of 150 sailor's lives. This responsibility was there, every minute of every day of my three-year command tour. Sailors, like other professions, get sick and can get hurt. At times, decisions needed to be made as to whether you aborted a mission to get a sailor off the ship or you tried to fix them with the minimal medical capability that you had on board. If you abort, and the sailor is not as bad as you had thought, your bosses question your decision making—and I would too. If you decide to cure the problem yourself, and God forbid the crew member gets worse or dies, your judgment will surely be questioned. On separate occasions, I have made both of these decisions, and I count myself among the very lucky to have chosen correctly.

I always knew that some bad decisions could mean life or death for everyone in that metal tube.

As I became more senior, I commanded a squadron of eight submarines. In that same assignment, my responsibilities included the development of the tactics that all the US Submarine Force would use in time of war. When I left that job, I was hoping that the Soviets were glad to see me go, hoping that the next guy was not going to be so tenacious. They were wrong.

At one time I commanded all the United States and NATO submarines in the Mediterranean Sea during the war in Yugoslavia. During this tour of duty, I found out just how difficult it can be to orchestrate forces that are supposed to be friends.

The communications capabilities of the various NATO countries are very different, with some verging on primitive. Hostile feelings between some allies were thousands of years old, and even though the members of these navies would smile at each other during the morning staff meeting, they were trying to undermine each other for the rest of the day. At times country A would refuse to relay country Bs communications, so it was hard to get the exact status of what was happening down range. There were even two country's submarine operating areas that had to be separated by distance, for fear that they would shoot at each other. The word "friend" did not mean the same as it had back in Nebraska.

My last tour of duty was as the Deputy Commander, United States Strategic Command at Offutt Air Force Base in Omaha. For me, this was "coming home." Thirty-seven years earlier, I had taken my Naval Academy entry physical at Offutt. Additionally, I would only be 130 miles from Fairbury, and I could regularly see my dad, who was still in good health. Unfortunately, my mother had passed. Too bad—I think Mom would have been very proud.

Of course, Dad had his own way of exerting pride. He had mellowed over the years, and you could tell by the smile on his face that maybe I had turned out OK after all. I hope he was taking credit for any success that I had, because he deserved it. The base guards would call me whenever Dad arrived for a visit. The guards would be laughing as they explained that Dad had a unique way of announcing his presence. He would drive up to the gate and in a very authoritative and loud fashion announce, "I'm the admiral's father, and I'm going to his office." Then he would drive off without acknowledgment from the guards. It's a good thing the guards got to know him—today he would get shot!

\* \* \*

So why am I telling the reader about all this superfluous stuff that happened well after my childhood? This book is supposed to be about youthful lessons— parables, in short-story fashion. Well, that is exactly why this epilogue is necessary.

Every day of my professional career, I was thankful that I was born and raised in the Midwest. I was thankful for a mother and father who would not accept excuses. I was thankful for the family-like atmosphere of a small town that allowed me to compete academically and athletically, and sometimes fail. I was thankful for my school teachers, coaches, and mentors who made sure I was towing the line. Trust me when I tell you, not all kids in this country are as lucky.

Every day of my career I made decisions that were based on lessons that I had learned in Fairbury, Nebraska, and on a farm in Mahaska, Kansas. For the most part, my decisions were good, but I made mistakes—sometimes, doozies. But I knew that my childhood had given me the tools necessary to succeed and to approach situations in a logical manner. I had been taught to be decisive in my decision making, but most of all, I had been taught—no, commanded—to listen.

I didn't know it at the time, but the most important thing that I learned in my childhood was to listen. Even when, as a kid, I was screwing around or joking, I was listening.

You can learn a lot from other people, good things and bad things, if you will just listen—I made a career of it. And it all started while observing the good, bad, and stupid things that happened in my childhood—parables.

# Acknowledgments

I would like to acknowledge many of the people who helped me remember these stories and then produce this document. My sisters, Judy and Debbie, were integral in helping me retrieve and catalogue pictures from old cardboard boxes in storage areas. My wife, Janet, was the perfect—and first—proofreader, who refereed how I should explain the various stories. And then, of course, there would be no "Parables" without my classmates. These wonderful old friends are the cast of characters that make the stories possible. They are the friends in my young life that taught me so many valuable lessons. Thank you, one and all.

Additionally, I want to thank all the folks at Infusionmedia, who took in a first-time author and so professionally led me by the hand. Cris Trautner and Aaron Vacin turned my primitive effort into a work that I could be proud of—they are the best.

# About the Author

Vice Admiral Dennis A. Jones, USN (Ret.), is a true Cornhusker. He was born and raised in Fairbury, Nebraska, and attended Fairbury Junior College for one year, followed by a year at the University of Nebraska in Lincoln. He was then appointed as a midshipman at the United States Naval Academy in Annapolis, Maryland, where he graduated and was commissioned as an officer in the Navy. Following graduation, he was selected for the Navy's very elite Nuclear Propulsion Training Program and then went on to submarine training. He also attended Harvard University, studying in the program for senior executives in national and international security affairs.

From the beginning of his training at the Naval Academy until he retired, he wore the uniform of his country for over thirty-seven years. He served on multiple submarines throughout his career and commanded the fast attack submarine USS *Birmingham* (SSN 695) during the height of the Cold War. Additionally, he was privileged to command a squadron of eight nuclear-powered submarines.

Admiral Jones served as commander of all the United States and NATO submarines in the Mediterranean Sea during the war in Yugoslavia.

His final tour of active service was as the deputy commander of United States Strategic Command (StratCom) at Offutt Air Force Base in Omaha. StratCom is responsible for all of the country's nuclear forces, weapons, and strategic operations supporting the national security objectives.

Following his retirement from active duty, Admiral Jones had a wonderful twelve-year second career as a vice president of a large defense-oriented corporation, L-3 Communications Corporation.

Admiral Jones and his wife, Janet, recently moved to North Carolina from the Washington, DC area. They are joined there in their retirement by the most wonderful dog in the world named Tallie and a mischievous black cat named Ruby.

The admiral describes his retirement as living in a state of "genteel poverty" while he works on completing items on his bucket list. Now that writing a book has been checked off the list, he is considering taking guitar lessons. His everyday mantra is "I have been very, very lucky in my life. Now I'm blessed to be surrounded by the people and animals that I love to help me enjoy the rest of the adventure."

*My official Navy photo.*

*My wife, Janet, who keeps everything together, and me.*

*Tallie and me.*